Addition and Subtraction Facts to 20

Jack has 11 . Jane has 7 .

1. How many more does Jack have than Jane?

    $11 - 7 = 4$ 4 more .

2. How many do they have in all?

    $11 + 7 = 18$ 18 in all.

HINTS:

- Read each problem carefully to see whether to add or subtract.
- Watch the sign.

Add or subtract.

①
$$\begin{array}{r} 1\,2 \\ +\quad 6 \\ \hline 18 \end{array}$$

②
$$\begin{array}{r} 1\,8 \\ -\quad 4 \\ \hline \end{array}$$

③
$$\begin{array}{r} 1\,5 \\ -\quad 7 \\ \hline \end{array}$$

④
$$\begin{array}{r} 1\,4 \\ +\quad 3 \\ \hline \end{array}$$

⑤
$$\begin{array}{r} 2 \\ +\,1\,6 \\ \hline \end{array}$$

⑥
$$\begin{array}{r} 1\,7 \\ -\quad 5 \\ \hline \end{array}$$

⑦ $9 + 5$ = _____

⑧ $11 - 6$ = _____

⑨ $16 - 12$ = _____

⑩ $8 + 6$ = _____

⑪ $3 + 15$ = _____

⑫ $19 - 8$ = _____

⑬ $20 - 7$ = _____

⑭ $7 + 6$ = _____

⑮ $2 + 8 + 5$ = _____

⑯ $4 + 2 + 7$ = _____

Write the missing numbers.

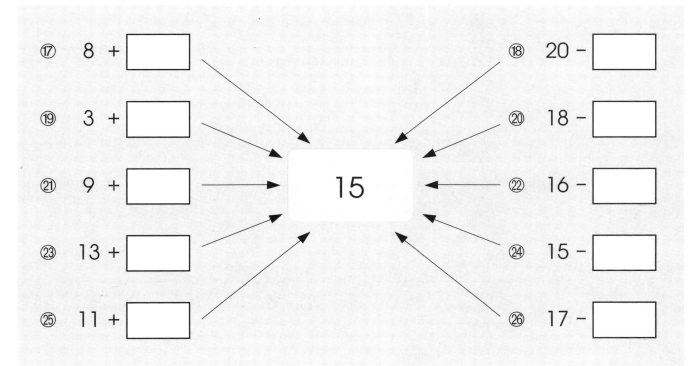

⑰ 8 + ☐

⑲ 3 + ☐

㉑ 9 + ☐

㉓ 13 + ☐

㉕ 11 + ☐

15

⑱ 20 − ☐

⑳ 18 − ☐

㉒ 16 − ☐

㉔ 15 − ☐

㉖ 17 − ☐

Fill in the ◯ with + or −.

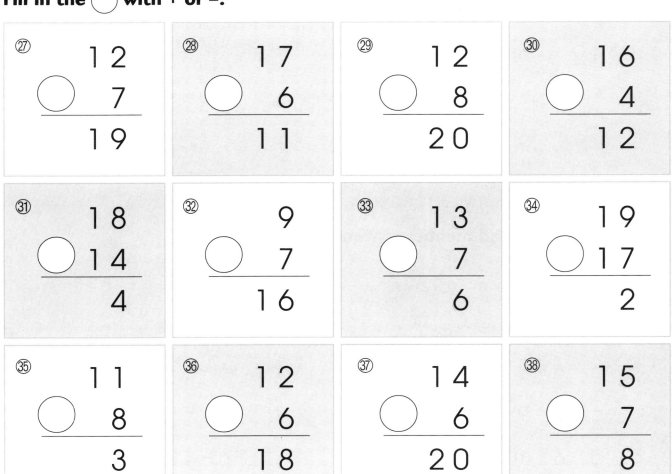

㉗
```
  1 2
◯  7
─────
  1 9
```

㉘
```
  1 7
◯  6
─────
  1 1
```

㉙
```
  1 2
◯  8
─────
  2 0
```

㉚
```
  1 6
◯  4
─────
  1 2
```

㉛
```
  1 8
◯ 1 4
─────
    4
```

㉜
```
  9
◯ 7
─────
1 6
```

㉝
```
  1 3
◯  7
─────
    6
```

㉞
```
  1 9
◯ 1 7
─────
    2
```

㉟
```
  1 1
◯  8
─────
    3
```

㊱
```
  1 2
◯  6
─────
  1 8
```

㊲
```
  1 4
◯  6
─────
  2 0
```

㊳
```
  1 5
◯  7
─────
    8
```

Colour the bones that match each number.

③⑨ **8**

| 12 – 6 | 18 – 10 | 6 + 2 |

④⓪ **13**

| 6 + 7 | 16 – 3 | 17 – 5 |

④① **17**

| 12 + 5 | 20 – 4 | 9 + 8 |

④② **12**

| 6 + 5 | 15 – 3 | 17 – 5 |

④③ **10**

| 19 – 8 | 3 + 7 | 16 – 6 |

Complete the related number sentences.

④④
6 + 6 = 12

a. 6 + 7 = _____

b. 6 + 8 = _____

c. 6 + 9 = _____

d. 6 + 10 = _____

④⑤
16 – 8 = 8

a. 16 – 7 = _____

b. 16 – 6 = _____

c. 16 – 5 = _____

d. 16 – 4 = _____

Complete.

㊻ Mom buys 12 red and 6 green .

How many does she buy in all?

_____ = _____ _____ in all.

㊼ There are 16 🍬 in the bag. Sue eats 12 🍬.

How many 🍬 are left in the bag?

_____ = _____ _____ 🍬 left.

㊽ There are 20 children in the class. 12 of them are boys.

How many girls are there in the class?

_____ = _____ _____ girls.

㊾ Sue has 10 red 🧱 and 5 green 🧱.

How many 🧱 does Sue have altogether?

_____ = _____ _____ altogether.

Count by 5's to help Little Bunny get the carrot. Draw the path.

20	25	30	55	60	90
5	20	45	50	65	100
10	15	40	35	70	95
5	20	35	80	75	100
10	25	30	85	90	95

More about Addition Facts

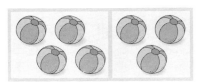 

4 + 3 = 7   3 + 4 = 7

4 + 3 = 3 + 4 = 7

HINTS:

- Even if the order of an addition changes, the answer is the same.

  e.g. 4 + 3 = 3 + 4 = 7

- Different addition sentences may give the same SUM.

  e.g. 2 + 3 = 1 + 4 = 5

Complete the related facts.

①
a.   2 + 3 = _____ 5

b.   3 + 2 = _____

c.   2 + 3 = 3 + 2 = _____

②
a.   5 + 3 = _____

b.   3 + 5 = _____

c.   5 + 3 = 3 + 5 = _____

③
a.    4 + 6 = _____

b.   6 + 4 = _____

c.   4 + 6 = 6 + 4 = _____

④
a.   0 + 5 = _____

b.   5 + 0 = _____

c.   0 + 5 = 5 + 0 = _____

⑤
a.   2 + 6 = _____

b.   6 + 2 = _____

c.   2 + 6 = 6 + 2 = _____

Write the missing numbers.

⑥ $3 + 8 \;= 8 +$ _____

⑦ $5 + 7 \;=$ _____ $+ 5$

⑧ $11 + 4 =$ _____ $+ 11$

⑨ $8 + 9 \;= 9 +$ _____

⑩ $10 +$ _____ $= 7 + 10$

⑪ $5 +$ _____ $= 6 + 5$

⑫   _____ $+ 12 = 12 + 6$

⑬   _____ $+ 4 = 4 + 13$

⑭ $14 + 6 =$ _____ $+ 14$

⑮ $17 + 2 = 2 +$ _____

Complete and match.

⑯ $10 + 8 \;=$ _____ $+ 10$ •   •   17

⑰ $12 + 5 \;=$ _____ $+ 12$ •   •   14

⑱ $4 + 15 \;= 15 +$ _____   •   •   18

⑲ $5 + 9 \;= 9 +$ _____   •   •   16

⑳   _____ $+ 6 = 6 + 14$ •   •   19

㉑ $3 +$ _____ $= 13 + 3$ •   •   20

Write different addition sentences for each sum.

㉒
a. _____ + _____ = 7

b. _____ + _____ = 7

c. _____ + _____ = 7

㉓
a. _____ + _____ = 6

b. _____ + _____ = 6

c. _____ + _____ = 6

㉔
a. _____ + _____ = 8

b. _____ + _____ = 8

c. _____ + _____ = 8

d. _____ + _____ = 8

㉕
a. _____ + _____ = 9

b. _____ + _____ = 9

c. _____ + _____ = 9

d. _____ + _____ = 9

㉖
a. 4 + _____ = 14

b. 5 + _____ = 14

c. 6 + _____ = 14

d. 7 + _____ = 14

e. 8 + _____ = 14

㉗
a. 9 + _____ = 17

b. 10 + _____ = 17

c. 11 + _____ = 17

d. 12 + _____ = 17

e. 13 + _____ = 17

The children are playing darts. Look at their scores. Complete each number sentence. Find their scores in the 2nd round.

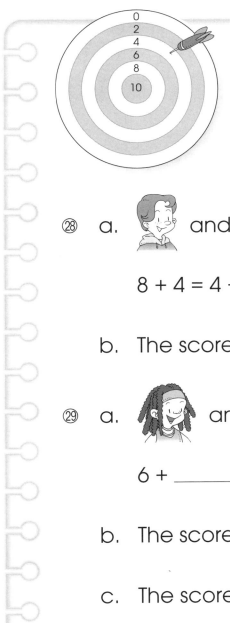

1st round	8	4	6	2
2nd round	4			

㉘ a. and have the same total score.

   8 + 4 = 4 + _____ = 12

   b. The score of in the 2nd round is _____ .

㉙ a. and have the same total score.

   6 + _____ = 2 + _____ = 8

   b. The score of in the 2nd round is _____ .

   c. The score of in the 2nd round is _____ .

Circle 6 pairs of numbers that give a sum equal to 11.

2	3	8	7	6	5	4
4	7	5	9	2	3	6
6	9	0	11	4	10	1

Relating Subtraction to Addition

$9 + 3 = 12$

$12 - 3 = 9$

$12 - 9 = 3$

HINTS:

A family of facts shows how numbers are related using + , − , =.

e.g. a family of facts of 4, 5 , 9 is

$4 + 5 = 9$
$5 + 4 = 9$
$9 - 4 = 5$
$9 - 5 = 4$

Count the items. Complete each number sentence.

① $4 + 8 =$ _____

$12 -$ _____ $= 8$

$12 -$ _____ $= 4$

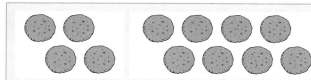

② $12 + 6 =$ _____

$18 -$ _____ $= 6$

③ $6 + 9 =$ _____

$15 -$ _____ $= 9$

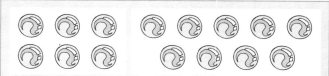

④ $9 + 8 =$ _____

$17 -$ _____ $= 9$

⑤ $5 + 6 =$ _____

$11 -$ _____ $= 5$

Complete each family of facts.

⑥   8   6   14

$$\underline{\quad 8 \quad} + \underline{\qquad} = \underline{\qquad}$$

$$\underline{\quad 6 \quad} + \underline{\qquad} = \underline{\qquad}$$

$$14 - \underline{\quad 8 \quad} = \underline{\qquad}$$

$$14 - \underline{\qquad} = \underline{\quad 8 \quad}$$

⑦   5   6   11

$$\underline{\qquad} + \underline{\qquad} = \underline{\qquad}$$

$$\underline{\qquad} + \underline{\qquad} = \underline{\qquad}$$

$$\underline{\qquad} - \underline{\qquad} = \underline{\qquad}$$

$$\underline{\qquad} - \underline{\qquad} = \underline{\qquad}$$

⑧   4   9   13

$$\underline{\qquad} + \underline{\qquad} = \underline{\qquad}$$

$$\underline{\qquad} + \underline{\qquad} = \underline{\qquad}$$

$$\underline{\qquad} - \underline{\qquad} = \underline{\qquad}$$

$$\underline{\qquad} - \underline{\qquad} = \underline{\qquad}$$

⑨   12   7   19

$$\underline{\qquad} + \underline{\qquad} = \underline{\qquad}$$

$$\underline{\qquad} + \underline{\qquad} = \underline{\qquad}$$

$$\underline{\qquad} - \underline{\qquad} = \underline{\qquad}$$

$$\underline{\qquad} - \underline{\qquad} = \underline{\qquad}$$

⑩   7   9   16

$$\underline{\qquad} + \underline{\qquad} = \underline{\qquad}$$

$$\underline{\qquad} + \underline{\qquad} = \underline{\qquad}$$

$$\underline{\qquad} - \underline{\qquad} = \underline{\qquad}$$

$$\underline{\qquad} - \underline{\qquad} = \underline{\qquad}$$

⑪   11   6   17

$$\underline{\qquad} + \underline{\qquad} = \underline{\qquad}$$

$$\underline{\qquad} + \underline{\qquad} = \underline{\qquad}$$

$$\underline{\qquad} - \underline{\qquad} = \underline{\qquad}$$

$$\underline{\qquad} - \underline{\qquad} = \underline{\qquad}$$

Write the missing numbers.

⑫

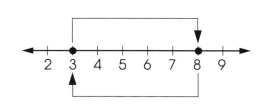

$$3 + \boxed{} = 8$$

$$8 - \boxed{} = 3$$

⑬

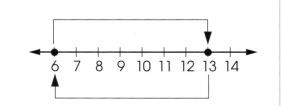

$$6 + \boxed{} = 13$$

$$13 - \boxed{} = 6$$

⑭

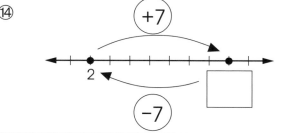

⑮

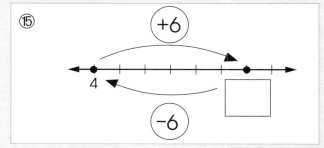

⑯

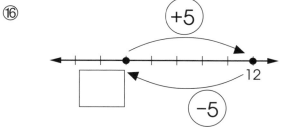

⑰

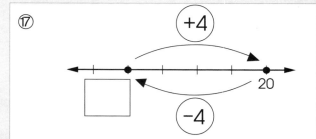

⑱

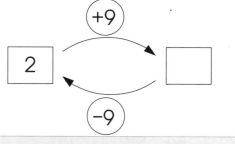

⑲

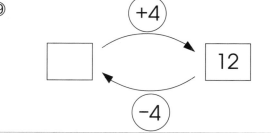

⑳

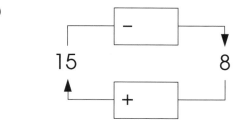

㉑

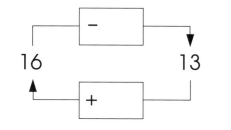

Use the family of facts. Fill in the missing numbers.

㉒ 4 + ☐ = 13
    13 − ☐ = 4

㉓ 9 + ☐ = 17
    17 − ☐ = 9

㉔ 6 + ☐ = 12
    12 − 6 = ☐

㉕ 7 + ☐ = 11
    11 − 7 = ☐

㉖ 7 + ☐ = 15
    15 − ☐ = 7

㉗ ☐ + 10 = 17
    17 − 10 = ☐

㉘
```
    8          1 3
 + ☐         - ☐
 ───         ───
  1 3          8
```

㉙
```
   2 0          ☐
 - ☐         + 1 1
 ───         ─────
  1 1         2 0
```

㉚
```
  1 4          ☐
 -   8       +   8
 ───         ─────
   ☐          1 4
```

㉛
```
   ☐          1 5
 +   9       - ☐
 ───         ───
  1 5           9
```

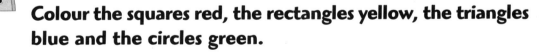

Colour the squares red, the rectangles yellow, the triangles blue and the circles green.

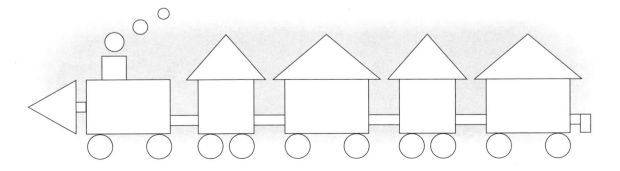

Adding and Subtracting Using Counting

4

1. 20 + 3 = 23 ← counting 3 forward from 20 gives 23

2. 30 − 6 = 24 ← counting 6 backward from 30 gives 24

HINTS:

- Count forward to find the sum of 2 numbers.
- Count backward to find the difference between 2 numbers.
- Use a number line or a number chart to help you count.

Find the sums or differences. Use the number line to help.

① 19 + 4 = _____

② 18 + 6 = _____

③ 25 − 4 = _____

④ 23 − 7 = _____

⑤ 29 − 5 = _____

⑥ 18 + 9 = _____

⑦ 16 + 6 = _____

⑧ 26 − 5 = _____

⑨ 27 − 8 = _____

⑩ 20 + 8 = _____

⑪ 30 − 12 = _____

⑫ 16 + 10 = _____

⑬ 22 + 7 = _____

⑭ 28 − 6 = _____

⑮ 17 + 9 = _____

⑯ 27 − 9 = _____

⑰ 24 + 6 = _____

⑱ 22 − 8 = _____

Add or subtract. Use the number chart to help.

51	52	53	54	55	56	57	58	59	60
61	62	63	64	65	66	67	68	69	70
71	72	73	74	75	76	77	78	79	80
81	82	83	84	85	86	87	88	89	90

⑲ 65 – 8 = _____

⑳ 78 – 11 = _____

㉑ 52 + 6 = _____

㉒ 68 + 7 = _____

㉓ 84 – 12 = _____

㉔ 81 + 8 = _____

㉕ 77 + 9 = _____

㉖ 90 – 11 = _____

㉗ 58 + 8 = _____

㉘ 62 – 6 = _____

㉙
```
   62
 –  1
```
[ ]

㉚
```
   70
 + 14
```
[ ]

㉛
```
   89
 – 10
```
[ ]

㉜
```
   69
 +  5
```
[ ]

㉝
```
   81
 +  7
```
[ ]

㉞
```
   90
 –  8
```
[ ]

㉟
```
   75
 – 20
```
[ ]

㊱
```
   63
 + 17
```
[ ]

Count and complete the addition sentences.

㉧ a.
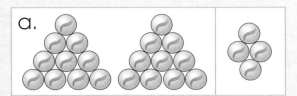

20 + _____ = _____

b.
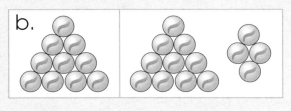

10 + _____ = _____

㊳ a.
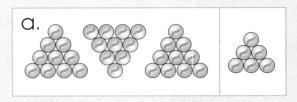

30 + _____ = _____

b.
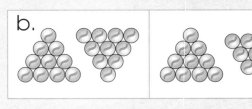

20 + _____ = _____

㊴ a.
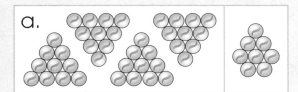

40 + _____ = _____

b.
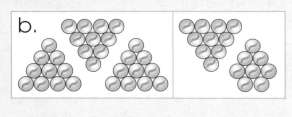

30 + _____ = _____

㊵ a.
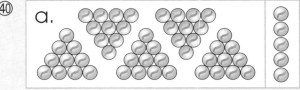

50 + _____ = _____

b.
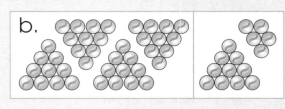

40 + _____ = _____

㊶ a.
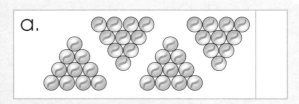

40 + _____ = _____

b.
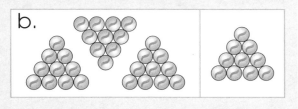

30 + _____ = _____

㊷ a.
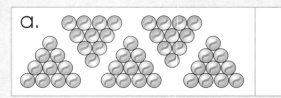

50 + _____ = _____

b.
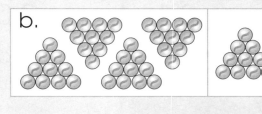

40 + _____ = _____

Cross out and count. Complete the subtraction sentences.

㊸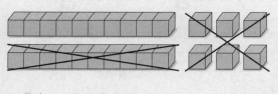

_26_ − 16 = _____

㊹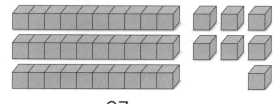

_____ − 27 = _____

㊺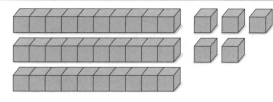

_____ − 14 = _____

㊻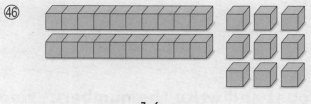

_____ − 16 = _____

㊼

_____ − 22 = _____

㊽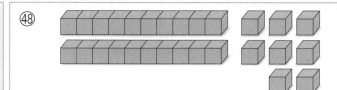

_____ − 15 = _____

㊾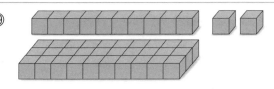

_____ − 31 = _____

㊿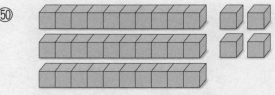

_____ − 12 = _____

 Just for Fun

Circle the shape in each group which does not belong.

①

②

Adding without Regrouping I

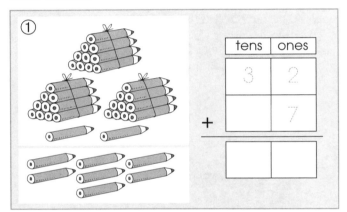

2 3 + 4 =   2 7

tens	ones
2	3
+	4
2	7

Count and write the numbers. Find the sums.

HINTS:

- Align the two numbers on the right-hand side.

  e.g.   23 + 4 = ?

tens	ones
2	3
+ 4	
6	3	✗

tens	ones
2	3
+	4
2	7	✓

  align the numbers on the right-hand side

- Add the ones first. Then add the tens.

①

tens	ones
3	2
+	7

②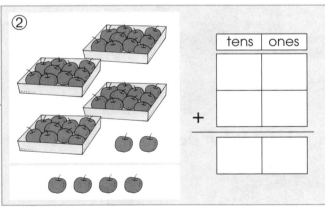

tens	ones
+	

③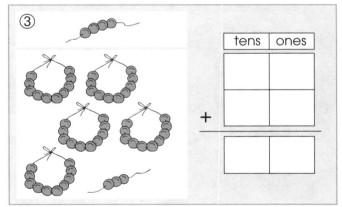

tens	ones
+	

④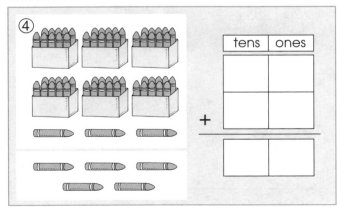

tens	ones
+	

⑤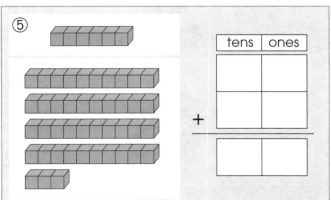

tens	ones
+	

Add.

⑥
```
    2 6
  +   3
  ┌─────┐
  └─────┘
```

⑦
```
    4 1
  +   8
  ┌─────┐
  └─────┘
```

⑧
```
      2
  + 3 6
  ┌─────┐
  └─────┘
```

⑨
```
    6 2
  +   6
  ┌─────┐
  └─────┘
```

⑩
```
      2
  + 5 5
  ┌─────┐
  └─────┘
```

⑪
```
    7 3
  +   4
  ┌─────┐
  └─────┘
```

⑫
```
    8 4
  +   5
  ┌─────┐
  └─────┘
```

⑬
```
    1 7
  +   2
  ┌─────┐
  └─────┘
```

⑭
```
    3 2
  +   6
  ┌─────┐
  └─────┘
```

⑮
```
      8
  + 5 1
  ┌─────┐
  └─────┘
```

⑯
```
    6 0
  +   7
  ┌─────┐
  └─────┘
```

⑰
```
    7 5
  +   3
  ┌─────┐
  └─────┘
```

⑱
```
    4 4
  +   4
  ┌─────┐
  └─────┘
```

⑲
```
    8 0
  +   6
  ┌─────┐
  └─────┘
```

⑳
```
    2 7
  +   2
  ┌─────┐
  └─────┘
```

㉑
```
      5
  + 9 0
  ┌─────┐
  └─────┘
```

㉒ $4 + 12 =$ _____

㉓ $31 + 7 =$ _____

㉔ $65 + 3 =$ _____

㉕ $42 + 6 =$ _____

㉖ $22 + 5 =$ _____

㉗ $4 + 52 =$ _____

㉘ $3 + 24 =$ _____

㉙ $15 + 3 =$ _____

Find the sums. Write the letters in ㊴ to solve the riddle.

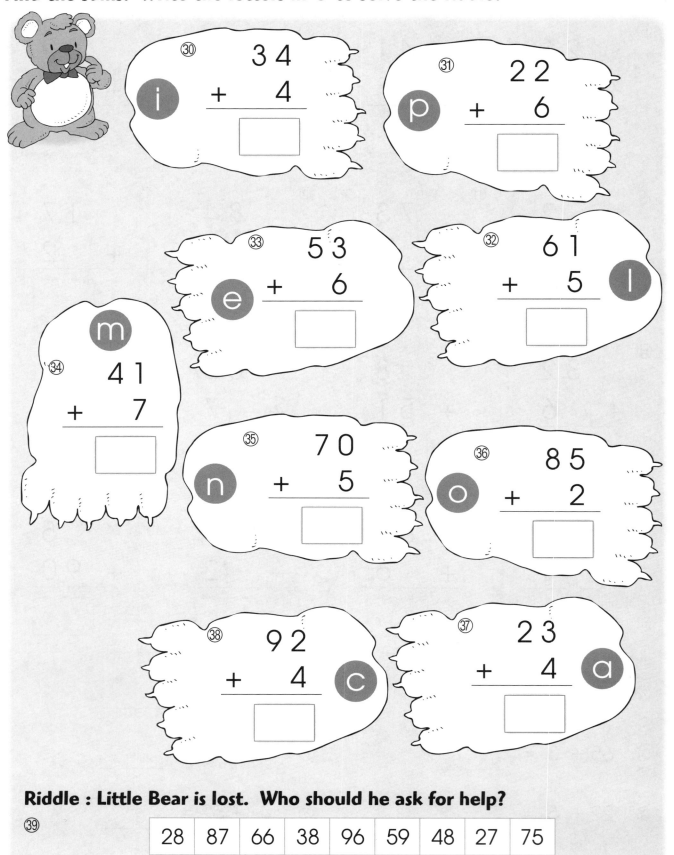

㉚ i
$$34 + 4$$

㉛ p
$$22 + 6$$

㉝ e
$$53 + 6$$

㉜ l
$$61 + 5$$

㉞ m
$$41 + 7$$

㉟ n
$$70 + 5$$

㊱ o
$$85 + 2$$

㊳ c
$$92 + 4$$

㊲ a
$$23 + 4$$

Riddle : Little Bear is lost. Who should he ask for help?

㊴

28	87	66	38	96	59	48	27	75

The | | | | | | | | .

Complete.

⑩ Sue has 32 . Sam gives Sue 4 more .

How many does Sue have in all?

_____ = _____   _____ in all.

④① There are 20 in the vase. Sue puts in 6 more .

How many are there in the vase altogether?

_____ = _____   _____ altogether.

④② Uncle Tom had 45 . 3 baby were born this morning.

How many does Uncle Tom have altogether?

_____ = _____   _____ altogether.

④③ Bob has 23 . He buys 6 more .

How many does he have in all?

_____ = _____   _____ in all.

Find the total score of each child in a computer game.

1st round	2 0	3	3 2	4
2nd round	8	2 4	7	1 5
Total score				

Adding without Regrouping II

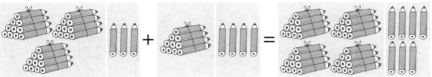

3 3 + 1 4 = 4 7

	tens	ones
	3	3
+	1	4
	4	7

Count and write the numbers.
Find the sums.

HINTS:

- Align the two numbers on the right-hand side.

  e.g.   23 + 14 = ?

tens	ones	← align on the right-hand
2	3	side
+ 1	4	

- Add the ones first. Then add the tens.

tens	ones		tens	ones
2	3		2	3
+ 1	4		+ 1	4
	7		3	7

  3 + 4 = 7   2 + 1 = 3

  23 + 14 = 37

①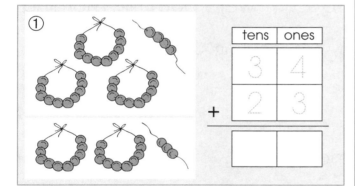

tens	ones
3	4
2	3
+	

②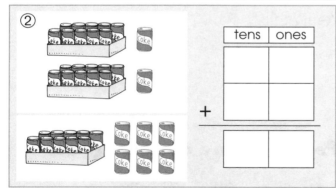

tens	ones
+	

③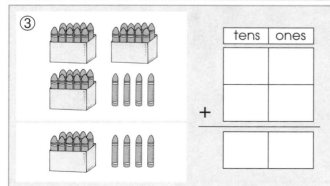

tens	ones
+	

④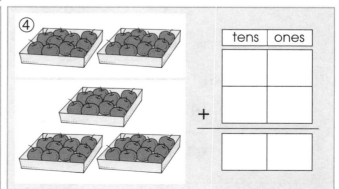

tens	ones
+	

Add.

⑤
```
   1 2
 + 2 6
 ┌─────┐
 │     │
 └─────┘
```

⑥
```
   3 4
 + 4 3
 ┌─────┐
 │     │
 └─────┘
```

⑦
```
   5 3
 + 1 4
 ┌─────┐
 │     │
 └─────┘
```

⑧
```
   6 1
 + 1 7
 ┌─────┐
 │     │
 └─────┘
```

⑨
```
   4 5
 + 2 2
 ┌─────┐
 │     │
 └─────┘
```

⑩
```
   1 5
 + 4 3
 ┌─────┐
 │     │
 └─────┘
```

⑪
```
   7 0
 + 2 1
 ┌─────┐
 │     │
 └─────┘
```

⑫
```
   8 2
 + 1 0
 ┌─────┐
 │     │
 └─────┘
```

⑬
```
   3 1
 + 1 6
 ┌─────┐
 │     │
 └─────┘
```

⑭
```
   2 0
 + 5 3
 ┌─────┐
 │     │
 └─────┘
```

⑮
```
   4 2
 + 3 6
 ┌─────┐
 │     │
 └─────┘
```

⑯
```
   5 4
 + 2 2
 ┌─────┐
 │     │
 └─────┘
```

⑰
```
   6 3
 + 3 0
 ┌─────┐
 │     │
 └─────┘
```

⑱
```
   4 4
 + 4 4
 ┌─────┐
 │     │
 └─────┘
```

⑲
```
   1 3
 + 3 3
 ┌─────┐
 │     │
 └─────┘
```

⑳
```
   2 5
 + 1 1
 ┌─────┐
 │     │
 └─────┘
```

㉑ 22 + 22 = _____

㉒ 16 + 31 = _____

㉓ 34 + 52 = _____

㉔ 40 + 28 = _____

㉕ 66 + 20 = _____

㉖ 73 + 15 = _____

㉗ 45 + 14 = _____

㉘ 84 + 12 = _____

Find the sums. Arrange the answers in correct counting order in ㊳, starting with the smallest number.

㉙ 34
 + 13

㉚ 12
 + 26

㉛ 28
 + 31

㉜ 26
 + 43

㉝ 42
 + 15

㉞ 51
 + 27

㉟ 53
 + 35

㊱ 38
 + 30

㊲ 60
 + 39

㊳

Complete the addition sentences.

㊴ Ben has 44 red and 32 green .

How many does he have in all?

_____ = _____ _____ in all.

㊵ There are 53 boys and 46 girls in the playground.

How many children are there in the playground?

_____ = _____ _____ children.

㊶ Dad planted 22 red and 36 yellow in the garden.

How many did Dad plant altogether?

_____ = _____ _____ altogether.

㊷ Sue has 15 . Sam has 30 .

How many do they have altogether?

_____ = _____ _____ altogether.

Colour the path with the correct answers. Help Sue find her story book.

34 + 25	⑷49	14 + 35	⑷48	25 + 32	⑸58	
⑸59		⑻86		⑹61		
15 + 42	⑸57	23 + 54	⑻87	34 + 42	⑺76	
⑷48		⑺77		⑹65		
26 + 41	⑹67	52 + 16	⑹68	30 + 35	⑺75	

Adding with Regrouping I

3 tens 4 ones + 8 ones = 3 tens 12 ones = 4 tens 2 ones

```
      tens  ones
        3    4
   +         8
   ─────────────
        4    2
```

Count and write the numbers.
Find the sums.

①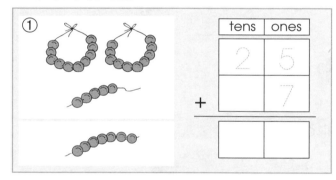

tens	ones
2	5
+	7

HINTS:

- Align the two numbers on the right-hand side.

  e.g. 34 + 8 = ?

  ```
  tens | ones        tens | ones
     3 | 4              3 | 4    ← align on the
   + 8 |              + 8 |        right-hand
       |      ✗           |        side
  ```

- Add the ones first.

  ```
  tens | ones       4 + 8
     3 | 4         = 12
   + | 8           = 1 ten + 2 ones
  ──────────        carry 1 ten to the tens column
       | 12         and leave 2 ones in the ones
                    column
  ```

- Then add the tens. Don't forget the 1 ten
  carried over from the ones column.

  ```
         1 ◄──────── carried over from the
                     ones column
  tens | ones
     3 | 4
   + | 8
  ──────────
     4 | 2
     ▲
     └──── 1 + 3 = 4
  ```

②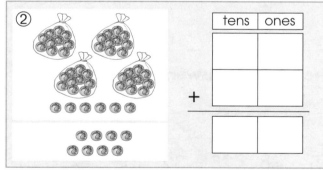

tens	ones
+	

③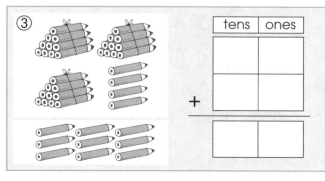

tens	ones
+	

④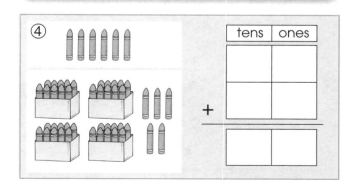

tens	ones
+	

Add. Remember to regroup.

⑤
```
   1 6
+    8
```
[ ]

⑥
```
   2 3
+    9
```
[ ]

⑦
```
   3 2
+    8
```
[ ]

⑧
```
   4 6
+    7
```
[ ]

⑨
```
     7
+  5 8
```
[ ]

⑩
```
   6 6
+    6
```
[ ]

⑪
```
   1 9
+    9
```
[ ]

⑫
```
   6 7
+    4
```
[ ]

⑬
```
   7 5
+    8
```
[ ]

⑭
```
   4 7
+    5
```
[ ]

⑮
```
     8
+  2 8
```
[ ]

⑯
```
   5 4
+    6
```
[ ]

⑰
```
   3 6
+    8
```
[ ]

⑱
```
   5 9
+    2
```
[ ]

⑲
```
   4 7
+    9
```
[ ]

⑳
```
     4
+  2 9
```
[ ]

㉑ 56 + 5 = _____

㉒ 37 + 7 = _____

㉓ 7 + 44 = _____

㉔ 26 + 9 = _____

㉕ 61 + 9 = _____

㉖ 73 + 8 = _____

㉗ 89 + 5 = _____

㉘ 3 + 37 = _____

Follow the path. Help Little Squirrel find its food.

㉙　36 + 7 = ☐

㉚　45 + 8 = ☐

㉛　$\begin{array}{r} 2\ 6 \\ +\quad 9 \\ \hline \square \end{array}$

㉜　57 + 3 = ☐

㉝　64 + 8 = ☐

㉞　$\begin{array}{r} 1\ 9 \\ +\quad 9 \\ \hline \square \end{array}$

㉟　74 + 9 = ☐

㊱　35 + 7 = ☐

㊲　$\begin{array}{r} 2\ 7 \\ +\quad 7 \\ \hline \square \end{array}$

㊳　84 + 6 = ☐

㊴　52 + 9 = ☐

㊵　$\begin{array}{r} 4\ 8 \\ +\quad 7 \\ \hline \square \end{array}$

㊶　65 + 5 = ☐

㊷　76 + 5 = ☐

Complete.

43 Bob has 18 . Ben gives Bob 6 more .
How many does Bob have in all?

_____ = _____   _____ in all.

44 Jack has 37 . Jane has 5 more than Jack.
How many does Jane have?

_____ = _____   _____ .

45 There are 28 in the garden. Mom plants 8 more .
How many are there in the garden altogether?

_____ = _____   _____ .

46 Sam has 45 . Jack gives him 9 more .
How many does Sam has altogether?

_____ = _____   _____ altogether.

The train must follow the path which contains addition with regrouping. Colour the path of the train.

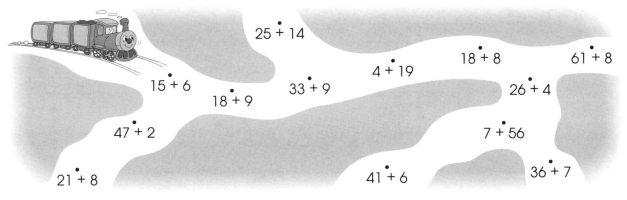

$25 + 14$

$18 + 8$ $61 + 8$

$4 + 19$

$15 + 6$ $33 + 9$ $26 + 4$

$18 + 9$

$47 + 2$ $7 + 56$

$21 + 8$ $41 + 6$ $36 + 7$

Adding with Regrouping II

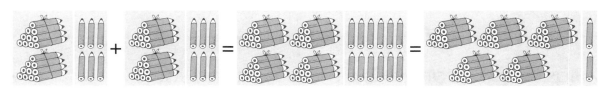

2 tens 6 ones + 2 tens 6 ones = 4 tens 12 ones = 5 tens 2 ones

```
    tens  ones
      2    6
   +  2    6
   ─────────────
      5    2
```

Count and write the numbers.
Find the sums.

①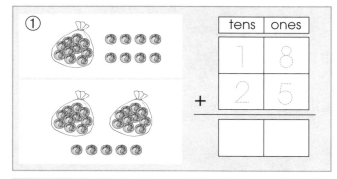

tens	ones
1	8
2	5

+

HINTS:

- Align the two numbers on the right-hand side.

  e.g. 26 + 26 = ?p

  ```
  tens   ones
    2     6    ← align on the right-hand
  + 2     6        side
  ```

- Add the ones first.

  ```
  tens   ones        6 + 6
    2     6      = 12
  + 2     6      = 1 ten + 2 ones
  ──────────
         12
  ```
  carry 1 ten to the tens column
  and leave 2 ones in the ones
  column

- Then add the tens.

  ```
      1  ←──────  carried over from the
  tens   ones      ones column
    2     6
  + 2     6
  ──────────
    5     2
  ```
  └─── 1 + 2 + 2 = 5

②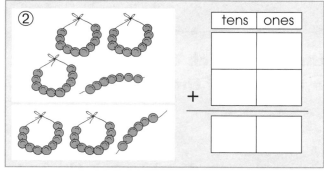

tens	ones

+

③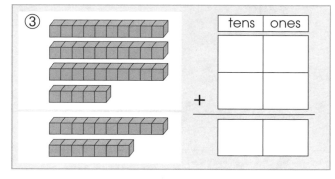

tens	ones

+

④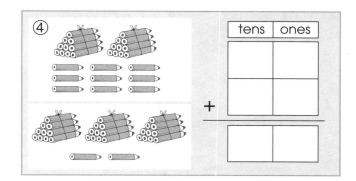

tens	ones

+

Add. Remember to regroup.

⑤
```
   3 7
 + 1 9
```
☐

⑥
```
   2 6
 + 3 8
```
☐

⑦
```
   4 3
 + 2 7
```
☐

⑧
```
   4 4
 + 3 8
```
☐

⑨
```
   6 4
 + 1 6
```
☐

⑩
```
   5 7
 + 2 6
```
☐

⑪
```
   3 2
 + 5 9
```
☐

⑫
```
   1 9
 + 4 4
```
☐

⑬
```
   2 7
 + 5 8
```
☐

⑭
```
   3 8
 + 4 6
```
☐

⑮
```
   5 6
 + 1 5
```
☐

⑯
```
   4 8
 + 4 8
```
☐

⑰
```
   6 3
 + 2 9
```
☐

⑱
```
   5 6
 + 3 9
```
☐

⑲
```
   1 5
 + 4 5
```
☐

⑳
```
   2 2
 + 4 8
```
☐

㉑ 18 + 65 = _____

㉒ 49 + 36 = _____

㉓ 43 + 38 = _____

㉔ 56 + 28 = _____

㉕ 24 + 69 = _____

㉖ 47 + 17 = _____

㉗ 55 + 27 = _____

㉘ 37 + 54 = _____

Colour the bookmarks that match each number.

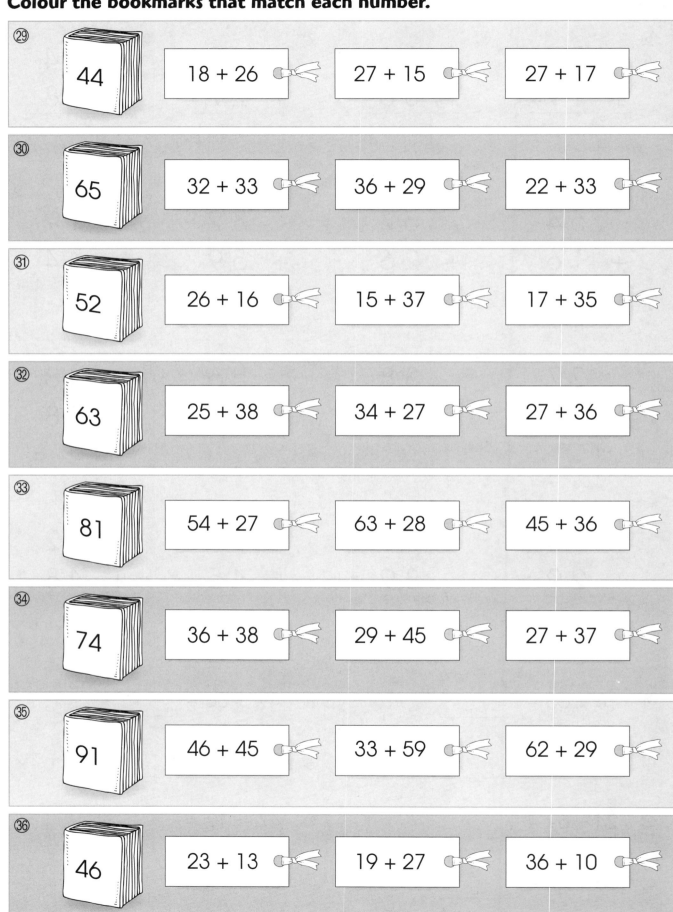

㉙ 44   18 + 26   27 + 15   27 + 17

㉚ 65   32 + 33   36 + 29   22 + 33

㉛ 52   26 + 16   15 + 37   17 + 35

㉜ 63   25 + 38   34 + 27   27 + 36

㉝ 81   54 + 27   63 + 28   45 + 36

㉞ 74   36 + 38   29 + 45   27 + 37

㉟ 91   46 + 45   33 + 59   62 + 29

㊱ 46   23 + 13   19 + 27   36 + 10

Complete.

㊲ There are 15 girls and 9 boys in the class.

How many children are there in the class altogether?

_____ = _____ _____ children altogether.

㊳ Bob has 36 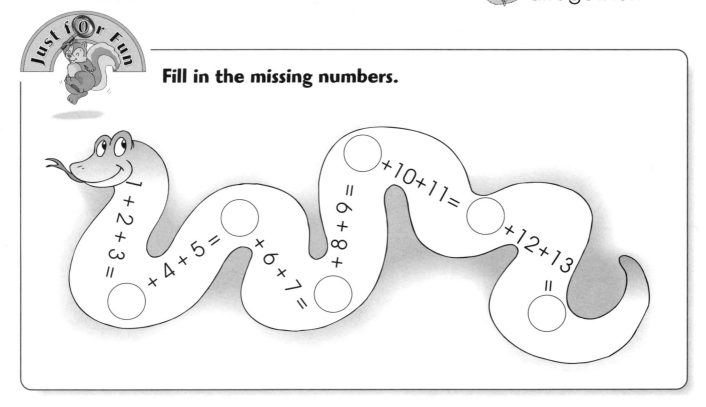 and Ben has 49 .

How many do they have altogether?

_____ = _____ _____ altogether.

㊴ The baker made 54 in the morning and 38 in the

afternoon. How many did the baker make in all?

_____ = _____ _____ in all.

㊵ There are 27 red and 45 yellow in the garden.

How many are there in the garden altogether?

_____ = _____ _____ altogether.

Just for Fun

Fill in the missing numbers.

1 + 2 + 3 = ◯

+ 4 + 5 = ◯

+ 6 + 7 = ◯

+ 8 + 9 = ◯

+ 10 + 11 = ◯

+ 12 + 13 = ◯

Midway

Complete the number sentences to show the related facts.

① 6 + 7 = _____ + 6 = _____   ② _____ + 6 = 6 + 5 = _____

③ 9 + 8 = 8 + _____ = _____   ④ 4 + 9 = _____ + 4 = _____

⑤ _____ + 5 = 5 + 7 = _____   ⑥ 3 + _____ = _____ + 3 = 11

⑦ 4 + _____ = 8 + 4 = _____   ⑧ 7 + _____ = _____ + 7 = 18

Write different addition sentences for each sum.

⑨
a. _____ + _____ = 10

b. _____ + _____ = 10

c. _____ + _____ = 10

d. _____ + _____ = 10

e. _____ + _____ = 10

⑩
a. 2 + _____ = 12

b. 3 + _____ = 12

c. 4 + _____ = 12

d. 5 + _____ = 12

e. 6 + _____ = 12

Complete each family of facts.

⑪

_8_ + _____ = _____

_7_ + _____ = _____

15 − _8_ = _____

15 − _____ = _8_

⑫

_____ + _____ = _____

_____ + _____ = _____

_____ − _____ = _____

_____ − _____ = _____

Write the missing numbers. Use the family of facts.

⑬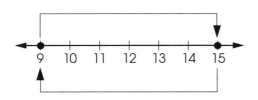

$9 + \boxed{} = 15$

$15 - \boxed{} = 9$

⑭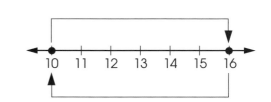

$10 + \boxed{} = 16$

$16 - \boxed{} = 10$

⑮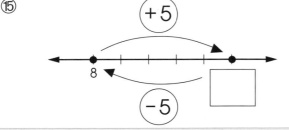

⑯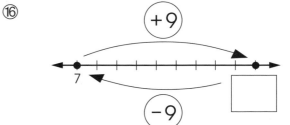

⑰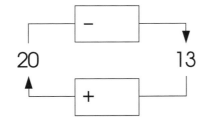

⑱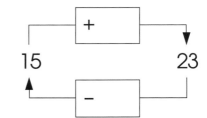

⑲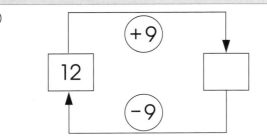

⑳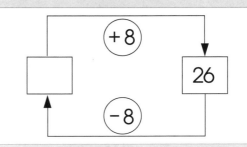

㉑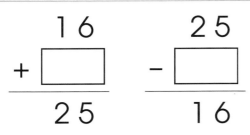

$16 + \boxed{} = 25$

$25 - \boxed{} = 16$

㉒

$21 - \boxed{} = 14$

$\boxed{} + 14 = 21$

Add or subtract.

㉓
```
   1 6
+    8
```
☐

㉔
```
   3 4
+    7
```
☐

㉕
```
   2 2
+  1 8
```
☐

㉖
```
   4 3
+  1 5
```
☐

㉗
```
   1 9
-    8
```
☐

㉘
```
   5 2
+  1 1
```
☐

㉙
```
   6 4
+  2 9
```
☐

㉚
```
   2 0
-  1 4
```
☐

㉛
```
   3 1
+  1 9
```
☐

㉜
```
   2 8
+  4 6
```
☐

㉝
```
   3 5
+  5 5
```
☐

㉞
```
   6 2
+  2 7
```
☐

㉟
```
     9
     6
+  1 3
```
☐

㊱
```
     7
     4
+  1 1
```
☐

㊲
```
     6
     8
+  1 6
```
☐

㊳
```
     8
     7
+  1 5
```
☐

㊴   64 + 15 = _____

㊵   47 + 28 = _____

㊶   39 + 23 = _____

㊷   72 + 9 = _____

㊸   8 + 41 = _____

㊹   26 + 59 = _____

㊺   13 + 43 = _____

㊻   18 − 11 = _____

Count Sue and Sam's cards, and answer the questions.

	35	23
	25	16

㊼ How many  do they have altogether? _______  altogether.	$\begin{array}{r} 35 \\ +\ 25 \\ \hline \end{array}$
㊽ How many cards does  have in all? _______ cards in all.	
㊾ How many cards does  have in all? _______ cards in all.	
㊿ How many  do they have altogether? _______  altogether.	

Subtracting without Regrouping I

tens   ones

      take away 4

tens	ones
3	8
–	4
3	4

38   –   4   = 34

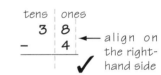

INTS:

- Align the numbers on the right-hand side.

  e.g. 38 – 4 = ?

tens	ones		tens	ones
3	8			3	8
– 4			–		4
X			**✓**	

  align on the right-hand side

- Subtract the ones first. Then subtract the tens.

tens	ones		tens	ones
3	8		3	8
–	4		–	4
	4		3	4

  8 – 4 = 4   3 – 0 = 0

Count and write the numbers. Find the differences.

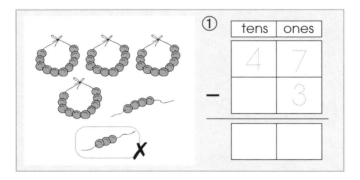

①
tens	ones
4	7
–	3

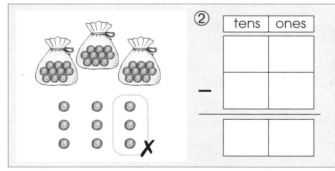

②
tens	ones
–	

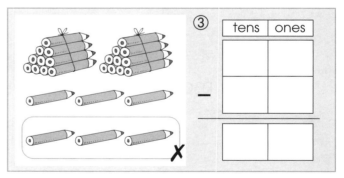

③
tens	ones
–	

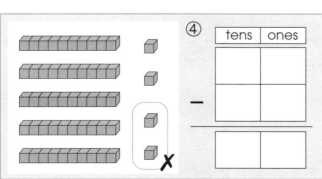

④
tens	ones
–	

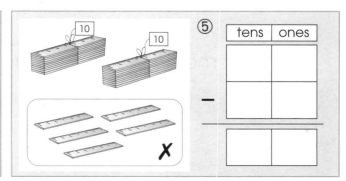

⑤
tens	ones
–	

Subtract.

⑥
```
   3 6
 -   5
 _____
```

⑦
```
   2 7
 -   6
 _____
```

⑧
```
   4 8
 -   5
 _____
```

⑨
```
   9 6
 -   4
 _____
```

⑩
```
   5 5
 -   3
 _____
```

⑪
```
   7 2
 -   2
 _____
```

⑫
```
   8 9
 -   7
 _____
```

⑬
```
   4 6
 -   3
 _____
```

⑭
```
   6 9
 -   3
 _____
```

⑮
```
   2 4
 -   3
 _____
```

⑯
```
   5 7
 -   2
 _____
```

⑰
```
   3 8
 -   7
 _____
```

⑱
```
   7 7
 -   5
 _____
```

⑲
```
   1 8
 -   6
 _____
```

⑳
```
   9 8
 -   5
 _____
```

㉑
```
   4 3
 -   3
 _____
```

㉒ 58 – 8 =

㉓ 29 – 5 =

㉔ 34 – 2 =

㉕ 66 – 4 =

㉖ 75 – 4 =

㉗ 87 – 3 =

㉘ 93 – 2 =

㉙ 41 – 1 =

Follow the path. Help Little Monkey get the coconuts.

㉚
```
   4 9
 -   5
 ─────
```

㉛
```
   3 6
 -   2
 ─────
```

㉜
```
   5 7
 -   4
 ─────
```

㉝
```
   6 5
 -   3
 ─────
```

㉞
```
   5 5
 -   5
 ─────
```

㉟
```
   3 9
 -   4
 ─────
```

㊱
```
   8 4
 -   3
 ─────
```

㊲
```
   9 3
 -   3
 ─────
```

㊳
```
   2 2
 -   1
 ─────
```

㊴
```
   8 4
 -   3
 ─────
```

㊵
```
   4 9
 -   8
 ─────
```

㊶
```
   3 7
 -   6
 ─────
```

㊷
```
   6 5
 -   2
 ─────
```

㊸
```
   6 6
 -   3
 ─────
```

㊹
```
   5 8
 -   6
 ─────
```

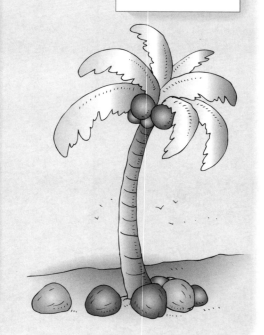

Complete.

50. There are 28  in the garden. Mom cuts 6 of them. How many  are left in the garden?

_____ = _____ _____  left.

51. Bob has 59 . He gives 5  to Ben. How many  does Bob have now?

_____ = _____ _____  .

52. Sue has 46 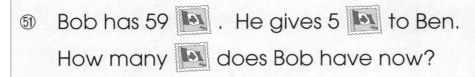. She has 4 more 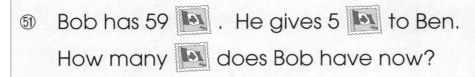 than Sam. How many 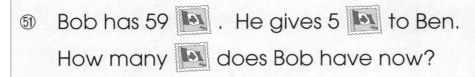 does Sam have?

_____ = _____ _____ 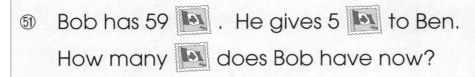 .

53. Uncle Tom has 37 . 3 of them burst. How many  does Uncle Tom have left?

_____ = _____ _____  left.

Count backward to find the gift for Sue. Draw the path.

16	14	13	14	3	2
20	15	12	11	4	1
19	16	14	10	3	2
18	17	8	9	4	5
19	18	7	6	5	6

Subtracting without Regrouping II

tens   ones

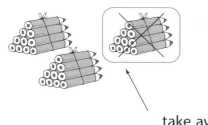

take away 15

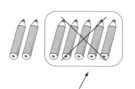

```
    tens  ones
      3    7
  -   1    5
  ─────────────
      2    2
```

$$37 - 15 = 22$$

Count and write the numbers. Find the differences.

HINTS:

- Align the numbers on the right-hand side.

  e.g. 37 – 15 = ?

  ```
  tens | ones
    3  |  7      ← align on the right-hand
  - 1  |  5          side
  ```

- Subtract the ones first. Then subtract the tens.

  ```
  tens | ones        tens | ones
    3  |  7            3  |  7
  - 1  |  5          - 1  |  5
  ─────────         ─────────
         2            2  |  2
       └ 7 – 5 = 2    └ 3 – 1 = 2
  ```

  37 – 15 = 22

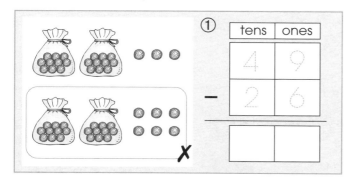

①
tens	ones
4	9
2	6

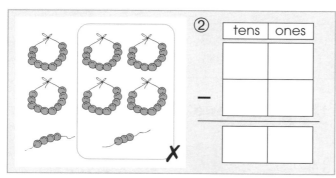

②
tens	ones

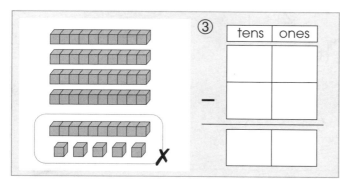

③
tens	ones

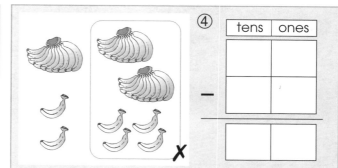

④
tens	ones

Subtract.

⑤
$$\begin{array}{r} 36 \\ -\ 12 \\ \hline \end{array}$$

⑥
$$\begin{array}{r} 48 \\ -\ 25 \\ \hline \end{array}$$

⑦
$$\begin{array}{r} 57 \\ -\ 33 \\ \hline \end{array}$$

⑧
$$\begin{array}{r} 65 \\ -\ 24 \\ \hline \end{array}$$

⑨
$$\begin{array}{r} 86 \\ -\ 54 \\ \hline \end{array}$$

⑩
$$\begin{array}{r} 74 \\ -\ 44 \\ \hline \end{array}$$

⑪
$$\begin{array}{r} 96 \\ -\ 65 \\ \hline \end{array}$$

⑫
$$\begin{array}{r} 29 \\ -\ 25 \\ \hline \end{array}$$

⑬
$$\begin{array}{r} 58 \\ -\ 37 \\ \hline \end{array}$$

⑭
$$\begin{array}{r} 66 \\ -\ 44 \\ \hline \end{array}$$

⑮
$$\begin{array}{r} 43 \\ -\ 31 \\ \hline \end{array}$$

⑯
$$\begin{array}{r} 84 \\ -\ 30 \\ \hline \end{array}$$

⑰
$$\begin{array}{r} 27 \\ -\ 12 \\ \hline \end{array}$$

⑱
$$\begin{array}{r} 33 \\ -\ 23 \\ \hline \end{array}$$

⑲
$$\begin{array}{r} 19 \\ -\ 15 \\ \hline \end{array}$$

⑳
$$\begin{array}{r} 78 \\ -\ 46 \\ \hline \end{array}$$

㉑ $45 - 22 \ = \ \boxed{}$

㉒ $99 - 77 \ = \ \boxed{}$

㉓ $76 - 30 \ = \ \boxed{}$

㉔ $54 - 14 \ = \ \boxed{}$

㉕ $69 - 58 \ = \ \boxed{}$

㉖ $25 - 11 \ = \ \boxed{}$

㉗ $37 - 21 \ = \ \boxed{}$

㉘ $83 - 70 \ = \ \boxed{}$

Find the differences. In each group, colour the balloons with the same answers.

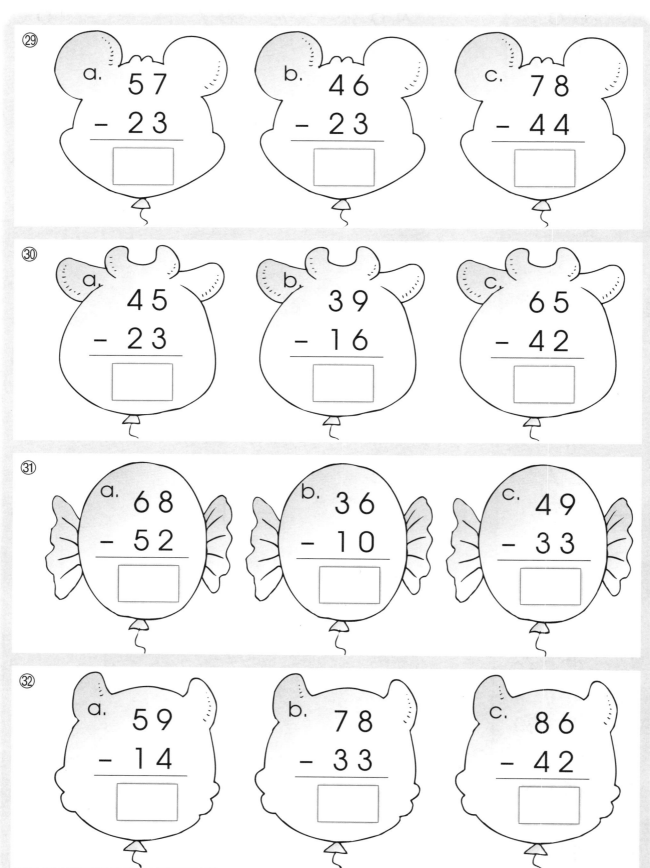

㉙ a.
$$57 - 23$$

b.
$$46 - 23$$

c.
$$78 - 44$$

㉚ a.
$$45 - 23$$

b.
$$39 - 16$$

c.
$$65 - 42$$

㉛ a.
$$68 - 52$$

b.
$$36 - 10$$

c.
$$49 - 33$$

㉜ a.
$$59 - 14$$

b.
$$78 - 33$$

c.
$$86 - 42$$

Complete.

㉝ Sue has 32 🪙 . Sam has 48 🪙 . How many more 🪙 does Sam have than Sue? _____ more 🪙 .	$\begin{array}{r} 4\ 8 \\ -\ 3\ 2 \\ \hline \end{array}$
㉞ There are 96 🌹 and 72 🌹 in the garden. How many more 🌹 are there than 🌹 ? _____ more 🌹 .	
㉟ There were 28 🐦 in a tree. 16 🐦 flew away. How many 🐦 were left in the tree? _____ 🐦 left.	
㊱ Jack has 67 🐚 . He gives Jane 35 🐚 . How many 🐚 does Jack have left? _____ 🐚 left.	

Just for Fun

Write the answers in the puzzle with one digit in each square.

Across
1. 84 – 23
3. 66 – 13
4. 57 – 20
5. 38 – 10
7. 26 – 16

Down
1. 98 – 34
2. 79 – 56
3. 89 – 32
4. 49 – 11
5. 56 – 32
6. 42 – 22

Subtracting with Regrouping I

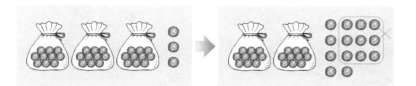

$$\begin{array}{r} {\scriptstyle 2 \quad 14} \\ \cancel{3}\ \cancel{4} \\ -\quad 9 \\ \hline 2\ 5 \end{array}$$

3 tens 4 ones = 2 tens 14 ones

   3 tens 4 ones – 9 ones
= 2 tens 14 ones – 9 ones
= 2 tens 5 ones

Regroup and Subtract.

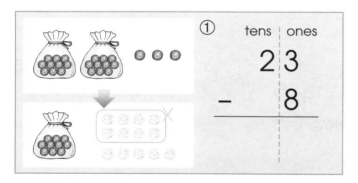

①
tens	ones
2	3
–	8

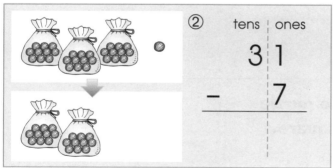

②
tens	ones
3	1
–	7

HINTS:

- Align the numbers on the right-hand side.

  e.g. 34 – 9 = ?

tens	ones
3	4
–	9

  ← align on the right-hand side

- Subtract the ones first. If you can't take away, borrow 1 ten from the tens column. Then subtract the tens.

  change 1 ten to 10 ones and leave 2 tens in the tens column →

  $$\begin{array}{r} {\scriptstyle 2 \quad 14} \\ \cancel{3}\ \cancel{4} \\ -\quad 9 \\ \hline 2\ 5 \end{array}$$

  ← 1 ten 4 ones = 14 ones

  ← 14 – 9 = 5

  └ 2 – 0 = 2

  34 – 9 = 25

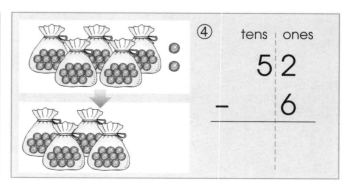

③
tens	ones
4	4
–	5

④
tens	ones
5	2
–	6

Subtract. Remember to regroup.

⑤
```
   6 3
 -   6
```
[ ]

⑥
```
   4 5
 -   8
```
[ ]

⑦
```
   3 4
 -   7
```
[ ]

⑧
```
   7 1
 -   9
```
[ ]

⑨
```
   2 7
 -   8
```
[ ]

⑩
```
   8 4
 -   9
```
[ ]

⑪
```
   5 6
 -   8
```
[ ]

⑫
```
   4 7
 -   9
```
[ ]

⑬
```
   9 0
 -   6
```
[ ]

⑭
```
   3 5
 -   9
```
[ ]

⑮
```
   7 2
 -   4
```
[ ]

⑯
```
   6 6
 -   8
```
[ ]

⑰
```
   4 3
 -   7
```
[ ]

⑱
```
   2 8
 -   9
```
[ ]

⑲
```
   8 1
 -   4
```
[ ]

⑳
```
   5 4
 -   6
```
[ ]

㉑ 33 − 8 = [ ]

㉒ 74 − 9 = [ ]

㉓ 60 − 5 = [ ]

㉔ 55 − 7 = [ ]

㉕ 81 − 6 = [ ]

㉖ 42 − 9 = [ ]

㉗ 22 − 7 = [ ]

㉘ 93 − 5 = [ ]

Subtract. Colour the lily pads if the answers are odd numbers. Help Little Frog find its Mom.

㉙
```
  3 2
-   9
-----
```

㉚
```
  5 3
-   8
-----
```

㉝
```
  2 5
-   7
-----
```

㉜
```
  2 3
-   6
-----
```

㉛
```
  4 6
-   9
-----
```

㉞
```
  6 4
-   9
-----
```

㉟
```
  7 1
-   8
-----
```

㊱
```
  6 1
-   7
-----
```

㊳
```
  3 7
-   9
-----
```

㊲
```
  3 5
-   6
-----
```

㊴
```
  4 0
-   7
-----
```

Complete.

④⓪ Jack had 25 . He ate 8 . How many were left?

_____ = _____   _____ left.

④① The baker made 52 . 9 were sold. How many  were left?

_____ = _____   _____ left.

④② Mom plants 40 in the garden. There are 7 less than . How many are there in the garden?

_____ = _____   _____ .

④③ Uncle Tom has 33 red . There are 6 more red than yellow . How many yellow does Uncle Tom have?

_____ = _____   _____ yellow .

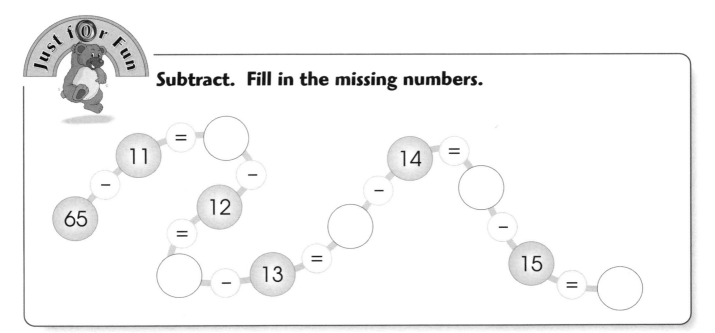

Subtract. Fill in the missing numbers.

Subtracting with Regrouping II

 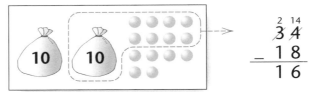

$$
\begin{array}{r}
\overset{2}{\cancel{3}}\ \overset{14}{\cancel{4}} \\
-\ 1\ \ 8 \\
\hline
1\ \ 6
\end{array}
$$

3 tens 4 ones – 1 ten 8 ones

= 2 tens 14 ones – 1 ten 8 ones

= 1 ten 6 ones

HINTS:

- Align the numbers on the right-hand side.

- Borrow 1 ten from the tens column and subtract the ones column first. Then subtract the tens column.

e.g.

tens	ones		tens	ones		tens	ones
3	4		$\overset{2}{3}$	$\overset{14}{4}$		$\overset{2}{3}$	$\overset{14}{4}$
– 1	8		– 1	8		– 1	8
				6		1	6

align the numbers $14 - 8 = 6$ $2 - 1 = 1$

so $34 - 18 = 16$

Regroup and subtract.

①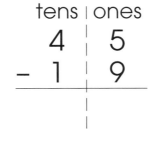

tens	ones
4	5
– 1	9

② 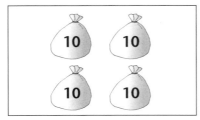 →

tens	ones
4	0
– 2	6

③ 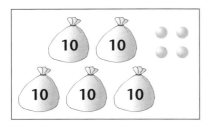 →

tens	ones
5	4
– 3	6

Subtract. Remember to regroup.

④
```
   4 3
 - 2 7
```

⑤
```
   5 6
 - 1 8
```

⑥
```
   3 5
 - 1 9
```

⑦
```
   7 0
 - 2 5
```

⑧
```
   6 1
 - 4 3
```

⑨
```
   8 4
 - 5 6
```

⑩
```
   2 7
 - 1 9
```

⑪
```
   4 6
 - 1 7
```

⑫
```
   7 2
 - 5 5
```

⑬
```
   3 3
 - 1 4
```

⑭
```
   8 5
 - 4 8
```

⑮
```
   9 6
 - 6 9
```

⑯
```
   5 4
 - 3 8
```

⑰
```
   4 0
 - 2 7
```

⑱
```
   2 5
 - 1 6
```

⑲
```
   6 5
 - 3 7
```

⑳ 31 – 14 = _____

㉑ 53 – 25 = _____

㉒ 64 – 39 = _____

㉓ 81 – 44 = _____

㉔ 93 – 46 = _____

㉕ 41 – 18 = _____

㉖ 71 – 59 = _____

㉗ 62 – 36 = _____

Subtract. Colour the eggs that match each number.

㉘   36

a.
$$\begin{array}{r} 6\ 3 \\ -\ 2\ 7 \\ \hline \end{array}$$

b.
$$\begin{array}{r} 5\ 2 \\ -\ 2\ 9 \\ \hline \end{array}$$

c.
$$\begin{array}{r} 5\ 2 \\ -\ 1\ 6 \\ \hline \end{array}$$

㉙   37

a.
$$\begin{array}{r} 6\ 3 \\ -\ 3\ 6 \\ \hline \end{array}$$

b.
$$\begin{array}{r} 7\ 4 \\ -\ 3\ 7 \\ \hline \end{array}$$

c.
$$\begin{array}{r} 9\ 6 \\ -\ 5\ 9 \\ \hline \end{array}$$

㉚   14

a.
$$\begin{array}{r} 4\ 1 \\ -\ 2\ 7 \\ \hline \end{array}$$

b.
$$\begin{array}{r} 6\ 0 \\ -\ 4\ 6 \\ \hline \end{array}$$

c.
$$\begin{array}{r} 5\ 3 \\ -\ 3\ 8 \\ \hline \end{array}$$

㉛   25

a.
$$\begin{array}{r} 8\ 3 \\ -\ 5\ 7 \\ \hline \end{array}$$

b.
$$\begin{array}{r} 4\ 3 \\ -\ 1\ 8 \\ \hline \end{array}$$

c.
$$\begin{array}{r} 6\ 2 \\ -\ 3\ 7 \\ \hline \end{array}$$

㉜   44

a.
$$\begin{array}{r} 7\ 2 \\ -\ 2\ 8 \\ \hline \end{array}$$

b.
$$\begin{array}{r} 6\ 3 \\ -\ 2\ 9 \\ \hline \end{array}$$

c.
$$\begin{array}{r} 8\ 0 \\ -\ 3\ 6 \\ \hline \end{array}$$

Complete.

③③ There are 92 children in the gym. 37 of them are boys. How many girls are there in the gym?

_____ = _____   _____ girls.

③④ At Sea World, Sue saw 43 on the rocks and 27 in the water. How many more were there on the rocks than in the water?

_____ = _____   _____ more .

③⑤ The baker made 55 in the morning and 39 in the afternoon. How many more did he make in the morning than in the afternoon?

_____ = _____   _____ more .

③⑥ There were 61 🥖 in the snack bar. 46 🥖 were sold. How many 🥖 were left?

_____ = _____   _____ 🥖 left.

Add or subtract. Write the letters to find what Sue wants to be.

19 + 27 = ⬜ I   73 − 48 = ⬜ E

52 − 36 = ⬜ R   25 + 46 = ⬜ S

44 − 27 = ⬜ G   4 + 9 + 26 = ⬜ N

A | 71 | 46 | 39 | 17 | 25 | 16 | .

Estimating Sums and Differences

23 ──── round to the nearest 10 ────→ 20   ∵ 3 is smaller than 5

36 ──── round to the nearest 10 ────→ 40   ∵ 6 is greater than 5

```
    2 3
  + 3 6
    5 9
```
↑
exact answer

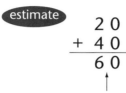 estimate

```
    2 0
  + 4 0
    6 0
```
↑
the sum is about 60

HINTS:

- Estimate by rounding all the numbers to the nearest 10.
- Rounding makes a number smaller or larger.
- To round to the nearest 10, look at the ones. If the digit is 5 or more, round up to the nearest 10; otherwise, round down.

The numbers are rounded to the nearest 10. Circle the correct answer.

① 27 ──────→   20   30

② 35 ──────→   30   40

③ 52 ──────→   50   60   ④ 44 ──────→   40   50

⑤ 63 ──────→   60   70   ⑥ 76 ──────→   70   80

⑦ 81 ──────→   80   90   ⑧ 93 ──────→   90   100

⑨ 38 ──────→   38   40   ⑩ 19 ──────→   10   20

Round each number to the nearest 10.

⑪ 31 _____	⑫ 22 _____	⑬ 49 _____
⑭ 58 _____	⑮ 13 _____	⑯ 84 _____
⑰ 7 _____	⑱ 46 _____	⑲ 11 _____
⑳ 69 _____	㉑ 95 _____	㉒ 4 _____

Estimate the sums. Compare the estimates with the exact answers.

㉓
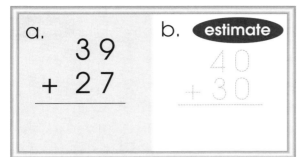
a.
$$39$$
$$+ 27$$

b. (estimate)
$$40$$
$$+ 30$$

㉔
a.
$$16$$
$$+ 28$$

b. (estimate)

㉕
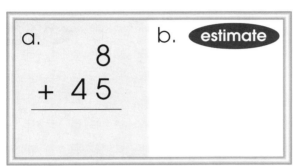
a.
$$8$$
$$+ 45$$

b. (estimate)

㉖
a.
$$51$$
$$+ 14$$

b. (estimate)

㉗
a.
$$26$$
$$+ 7$$

b. (estimate)

㉘
a.
$$34$$
$$+ 55$$

b. (estimate)

㉙ a. 73 + 19 = _____

(estimate)

b. _____ + _____ = _____

㉚ a. 22 + 66 = _____

(estimate)

b. _____ + _____ = _____

㉛ a. 33 + 46 = _____

(estimate)

b. _____ + _____ = _____

㉜ a. 51 + 44 = _____

(estimate)

b. _____ + _____ = _____

㉝ a. 64 + 27 = _____

(estimate)

b. _____ + _____ = _____

㉞ a. 13 + 45 = _____

(estimate)

b. _____ + _____ = _____

Estimate the differences. Compare the estimates with the exact answers.

㉟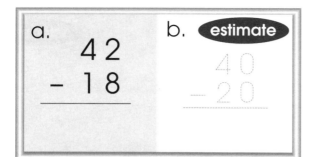

㊱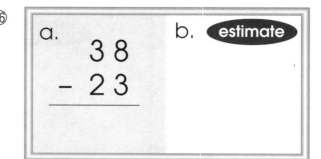

㊲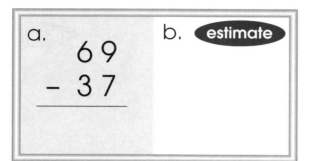

㊳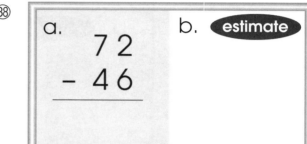

㊴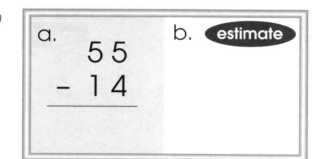

㊵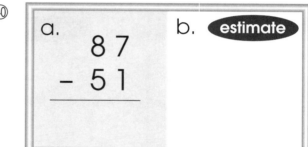

㊶ a. 93 – 46 = _____

   estimate

   b. _____ – _____ = _____

㊷ a. 46 – 13 = _____

   estimate

   b. _____ – _____ = _____

㊸ a. 75 – 27 = _____

   estimate

   b. _____ – _____ = _____

㊹ a. 64 – 19 = _____

   estimate

   b. _____ – _____ = _____

㊺ a. 82 – 34 = _____

   estimate

   b. _____ – _____ = _____

㊻ a. 36 – 8 = _____

   estimate

   b. _____ – _____ = _____

Estimate the sums or differences. Circle the correct descriptions.

㊼ 43 – 9

more than 30	less than 30

㊽ 25 + 47

more than 80	less than 80

㊾ 33 + 58

more than 90	less than 90

㊿ 62 – 44

more than 20	less than 20

(51) 95 – 57

more than 40	less than 40

(52) 19 + 54

more than 70	less than 70

Join the numbers.

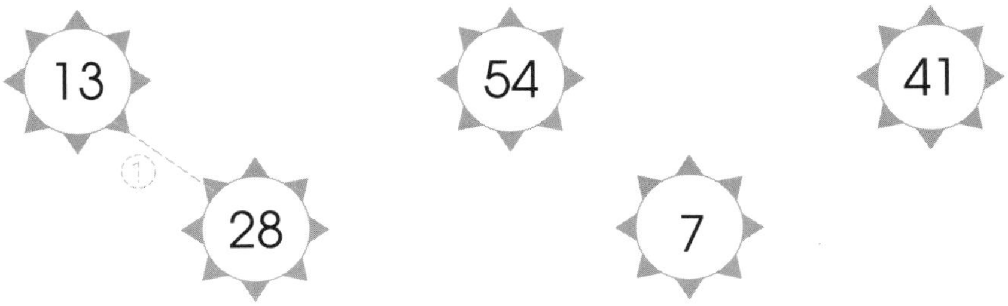

13 54 41

28 7

① Join 2 numbers that give a sum of about 40.

② Join 2 numbers that give a difference of about 30.

③ Join 2 numbers that give a sum of about 60.

④ Join 2 numbers that give a difference of about 20.

⑤ Join 2 numbers that give a sum of about 80.

⑥ Join 2 numbers that give a difference of about 40.

Checking Subtraction by Using Addition

Farmer Joe had 89 . 52 were sold. How many were left?

```
   8 9
 - 5 2
   3 7
```

check
```
   3 7
 + 5 2
   8 9
```

37 were left.

HINTS:

- Recall the family of facts,

  e.g. $5 + 4 = 9$

  $4 + 5 = 9$

  $9 - 5 = 4$

  $9 - 4 = 5$

- Check your subtraction by using addition.

  e.g.
  ```
      4 1  same      2 6
    - 1 5          + 1 5
      2 6            4 1
  ```
  The answer is right.

  ```
      4 1  not the      3 6
    - 1 5    same      + 1 5
      3 6              5 1
  ```
  The answer is wrong.

Do the subtraction and check the answers .

①
a.
```
   2 8
 - 1 6
```
☐

b. check ☐
```
 + 1 6
```
☐

②
a.
```
   6 3
 - 3 7
```
☐

b. check ☐
```
 + 3 7
```
☐

③
a.
```
   4 8
 - 2 6
```
☐

b. check ☐
```
 + 2 6
```
☐

④
a.
```
   5 1
 - 3 3
```
☐

b. check ☐
```
 + 3 3
```
☐

⑤
a.
```
   7 7
 - 4 2
```
☐

b. check ☐
```
 + 4 2
```
☐

⑥
a.
```
   8 2
 - 5 9
```
☐

b. check ☐
```
 + 5 9
```
☐

Subtract and check your answers.

⑦ a. 52 – 8 = _____

check

b. _____ + _____ = _____

⑧ a. 39 – 17 = _____

check

b. _____ + _____ = _____

⑨ a. 45 – 23 = _____

check

b. _____ + _____ = _____

⑩ a. 66 – 39 = _____

check

b. _____ + _____ = _____

⑪ a. 87 – 45 = _____

check

b. _____ + _____ = _____

⑫ a. 23 – 16 = _____

check

b. _____ + _____ = _____

⑬ a. 71 – 33 = _____

check

b. _____ + _____ = _____

⑭ a. 98 – 63 = _____

check

b. _____ + _____ = _____

⑮ a. 32 – 14 = _____

check

b. _____ + _____ = _____

⑯ a. 27 – 6 = _____

check

b. _____ + _____ = _____

⑰ a. 56 – 31 = _____

check

b. _____ + _____ = _____

⑱ a. 45 – 29 = _____

check

b. _____ + _____ = _____

Subtract. Complete 1 addition sentence and 1 subtraction sentence to check each answer.

⑲ a. 63 – 24 = _____

    check

    b. _____ + _24_ = _63_

    c. _63_ – _____ = _24_

⑳ a. 38 – 17 = _____

    check

    b. _____ + _____ = _____

    c. _____ – _____ = _____

㉑ a. 49 – 32 = _____

    check

    b. _____ + _____ = _____

    c. _____ – _____ = _____

㉒ a. 51 – 25 = _____

    check

    b. _____ + _____ = _____

    c. _____ – _____ = _____

㉓ a. 22 – 9 = _____

    check

    b. _____ + _____ = _____

    c. _____ – _____ = _____

㉔ a. 86 – 15 = _____

    check

    b. _____ + _____ = _____

    c. _____ – _____ = _____

㉕ a. 90 – 65 = _____

    check

    b. _____ + _____ = _____

    c. _____ – _____ = _____

㉖ a. 75 – 48 = _____

    check

    b. _____ + _____ = _____

    c. _____ – _____ = _____

Complete and check.

㉗ There are 56  and 39 in the pond. How many more are there than ?

[ ] – [ ] = [ ]

[ ] more .

Check

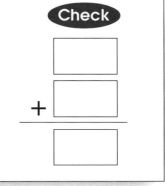

+ [ ]
[ ]
‾‾‾‾
[ ]

㉘ There are 48  and 26 in the pond. How many more are there than ?

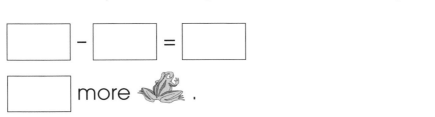

[ ] – [ ] = [ ]

[ ] more .

Check

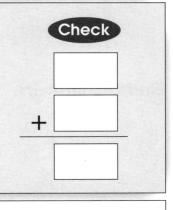

+ [ ]
[ ]
‾‾‾‾
[ ]

㉙ 15 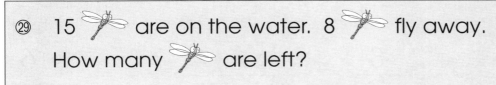 are on the water. 8 fly away. How many are left?

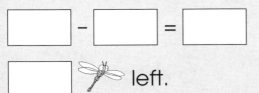

[ ] – [ ] = [ ]

[ ] left.

Check

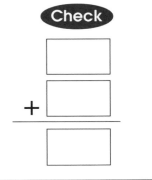

+ [ ]
[ ]
‾‾‾‾
[ ]

Just for Fun

Fill in the missing numbers.

① 15 _____ 25 30 _____ 40 _____

② 36 38 _____ 42 _____ _____ 48

③ 30 _____ _____ 60 70 _____ 90

More Addition and Subtraction

1. $17 + 9 - 16 = 26 - 16 = 10$
    └─── do the addition first

2. $33 - 19 + 27 = 14 + 27 = 41$
    └─── do the subtraction first

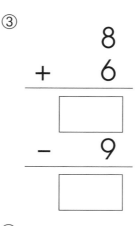

HINTS:

- To solve a problem with addition and subtraction, follow the order of the + and – signs in the problem to do the addition and subtraction.

- Knowing the patterns may help you find the sums or differences faster.

Find the answers. Be careful with the signs.

①
```
    4
+   5
─────
[     ]
-   3
─────
[     ]
```

②
```
    7
-   5
─────
[     ]
+   8
─────
[     ]
```

③
```
    8
+   6
─────
[     ]
-   9
─────
[     ]
```

④
```
   14
-   8
─────
[     ]
+   6
─────
[     ]
```

⑤
```
   32
-  16
─────
[     ]
-  14
─────
[     ]
```

⑥
```
   23
+  12
─────
[     ]
-   6
─────
[     ]
```

⑥
```
   54
+  28
─────
[     ]
-   2
─────
[     ]
```

⑧
```
   56
-  27
─────
[     ]
+   7
─────
[     ]
```

⑨ $45 + 25 - 18$

= _____ – 18

= _____

⑩ $27 + 53 - 46$

= _____ – 46

= _____

Add.

⑪ 10 + 30 = _40_   ⑫ 40 + 20 = _____

⑬ 16 + 20 = _____   ⑭ 20 + 26 = _____

⑮ 16 + 10 + 10 = _____   ⑯ 10 + 10 + 26 = _____

⑰ 9 + 4 = 10 + _3_

= _____

⑱ 19 + 25 = 20 + _____ = _____

⑲ 29 + 33 = 30 + _____ = _____

⑳ 18 + 35 = 20 + _____ = _____

㉑ 38 + 16 = 40 + _____ = _____

㉒ 4 + 8 = _____ + 10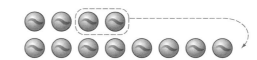

= _____

㉓ 22 + 18 = _____ + 20 = _____

㉔ 21 + 19 = _____ + 20 = _____

㉕ 16 + 28 = _____ + 30 = _____

㉖ 13 + 29 = _____ + 30 = _____

Subtract.

㉗ 50 − 20 = _____

㉘ 36 − 26 = _____

㉙ 64 − 20 = _____

㉚ 53 − 13 = _____

㉛ 73 − 30 = _____

㉜ 48 − 28 = _____

㉝ 60 − 30 = _____

㉞ 76 − 50 = _____

㉟ 87 − 57 = _____

㊱ 38 − 20 = _____

㊲ 49 − 29 = _____

㊳ 96 − 66 = _____

㊴ a. 8 − 5 = _____

b. 18 − 5 = _____

c. 28 − 5 = _____

d. 38 − 5 = _____

e. 48 − 5 = _____

㊵ a. 14 − 8 = _____

b. 24 − 8 = _____

c. 34 − 8 = _____

d. 44 − 8 = _____

e. 54 − 8 = _____

㊶ a. 72 − 8 = _____

b. 72 − 18 = _____

c. 72 − 28 = _____

d. 72 − 38 = _____

e. 72 − 48 = _____

㊷ a. 67 − 9 = _____

b. 67 − 19 = _____

c. 67 − 29 = _____

d. 67 − 39 = _____

e. 67 − 49 = _____

The children are playing with the spinner. Look at the children's scores in 3 rounds of the game. Find their final scores.

	1st round	2nd round	3rd round
	8	4	−5
	9	−3	5
	7	6	−4

43 The final score of is :

_____ = _____

44 The final score of is :

_____ = _____

45 The final score of is :

_____ = _____

Colour the correct answers to help Sue find her gift.

8 + 3 + 5

4 + 7 − 6

9 − 3 + 5

7 + 9 − 8

8 − 6 + 7

7 − 2 − 4

Addition and Subtraction with Money

How many cents does Sam have?

$$25¢ + 10¢ + 1¢ = 36¢$$

Sam has 36¢.

HINTS:

- $ means dollar.

- 1 loonie = $1   1 quarter = 25¢

   1 dime = 10¢   1 nickel = 5¢

   1 penny = 1¢

- $1 = 100¢

- Don't forget to use the ¢ sign when you add or subtract cents.

How many cents are in each set?

①  ☐ ¢

②  ☐ ¢

③  ☐ ¢

④  ☐ ¢

⑤  ☐ ¢

Which set gives a total of 100¢? Put a ✓ in the box.

⑥  ☐

⑦  ☐

How much change does Sue get?

	Sue has	Sue buys	Change Sue gets
⑧		49¢	_____ ¢ – _____ ¢ = _____ ¢
⑨		85¢	_____ ¢ – _____ ¢ = _____ ¢
⑩		36¢	_____ ¢ – _____ ¢ = _____ ¢
⑪		56¢	_____ ¢ – _____ ¢ = _____ ¢

How much more does Sam need?

	Sam has	Sam wants to buy	Extra amount Sam needs
⑫		67¢	_____ ¢ – _____ ¢ = _____ ¢
⑬		76¢	_____ ¢ – _____ ¢ = _____ ¢
⑭		72¢	_____ ¢ – _____ ¢ = _____ ¢
⑮		28¢	_____ ¢ – _____ ¢ = _____ ¢

Pay with the least number of coins. Write the number of each coin needed.

	25¢	10¢	5¢	1¢
⑯ pen 54¢				
⑰ ERASER 22¢				
⑱ pencils 80¢				
⑲ ruler 47¢				
⑳ sharpener 36¢				

Write each price. Then solve the problems.

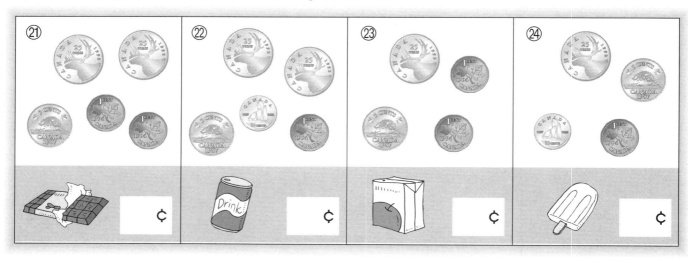

㉑ chocolate ____¢

㉒ Drink ____¢

㉓ juice box ____¢

㉔ popsicle ____¢

㉕ Sue has 100¢. She buys a [Drink]. How much does Sue have left?

$$\begin{array}{r} 100 \\ -\ 66 \\ \hline \end{array}$$

_____ ¢ left.

㉖ Sam buys a ▨ and a 🍦. How much does Sam pay in all?

_____ ¢ in all.

㉗ Jack buys a ▨ and a ▢. How much does Jack pay in all?

_____ ¢ in all.

㉘ Ben buys a Drink. Bob buys a ▢. How much more does Ben pay than Bob?

_____ ¢ more.

㉙ Sue buys a Drink. Jane buys a 🍦. How much less does Jane pay than Sue?

_____ ¢ less.

Just for Fun

Sam has 90¢. Put a ✓ in the ☐ to show what he can buy.

| ① ▨ + 🍦 ☐ | ② ▨ + ▢ ☐ |
| ③ Drink + ▢ ☐ | ④ ▢ + 🍦 ☐ |

Final

Add or subtract.

①
$$\begin{array}{r} 3\,2 \\ +\quad 9 \\ \hline \end{array}$$

②
$$\begin{array}{r} 2\,8 \\ +\,1\,7 \\ \hline \end{array}$$

③
$$\begin{array}{r} 3\,6 \\ -\quad 4 \\ \hline \end{array}$$

④
$$\begin{array}{r} 5\,2 \\ -\quad 9 \\ \hline \end{array}$$

⑤
$$\begin{array}{r} 7\,9 \\ -\,5\,1 \\ \hline \end{array}$$

⑥
$$\begin{array}{r} 8\,4 \\ -\,6\,6 \\ \hline \end{array}$$

⑦
$$\begin{array}{r} 4\,9 \\ +\quad 8 \\ \hline \end{array}$$

⑧
$$\begin{array}{r} 2\,1 \\ +\,4\,5 \\ \hline \end{array}$$

⑨
$$\begin{array}{r} 4\,6 \\ +\,2\,5 \\ \hline \end{array}$$

⑩
$$\begin{array}{r} 9\,2 \\ -\,3\,7 \\ \hline \end{array}$$

⑪
$$\begin{array}{r} 1\,8 \\ +\,6\,2 \\ \hline \end{array}$$

⑫
$$\begin{array}{r} 6\,0 \\ -\,4\,1 \\ \hline \end{array}$$

⑬
$$\begin{array}{r} 5\,8 \\ -\,2\,2 \\ \hline \end{array}$$

⑭
$$\begin{array}{r} 1\,4 \\ +\,5\,5 \\ \hline \end{array}$$

⑮
$$\begin{array}{r} 7\,3 \\ -\,3\,0 \\ \hline \end{array}$$

⑯
$$\begin{array}{r} 2\,3 \\ +\,4\,7 \\ \hline \end{array}$$

⑰ $27 + 46 =$ _____

⑱ $83 - 56 =$ _____

⑲ $65 - 49 =$ _____

⑳ $34 + 57 =$ _____

㉑ $47 + 9 \ =$ _____

㉒ $58 - 16 =$ _____

㉓ $63 - 38 =$ _____

㉔ $42 + 7 \ =$ _____

Estimate the sums or differences by rounding the numbers to the nearest 10. Compare the estimates with the exact answers.

㉕ a.
$$\begin{array}{r} 27 \\ +\ 36 \\ \hline \end{array}$$
b. estimate

㉖ a.
$$\begin{array}{r} 43 \\ -\ 26 \\ \hline \end{array}$$
b. estimate

㉗ a. 69 – 43 = ______

estimate

b. ______________ = ______

㉘ a. 42 + 16 = ______

estimate

b. ______________ = ______

Subtract. Check the answers using addition.

㉙ a.
$$\begin{array}{r} 37 \\ -\ 14 \\ \hline \end{array}$$
b. check

㉚ a.
$$\begin{array}{r} 52 \\ -\ 29 \\ \hline \end{array}$$
b. check

㉛ a. 64 – 48 = ______

check

b. ______________ = ______

㉜ a. 79 – 33 = ______

check

b. ______________ = ______

㉝ a. 86 – 54 = ______

check

b. ______________ = ______

㉞ a. 53 – 28 = ______

check

b. ______________ = ______

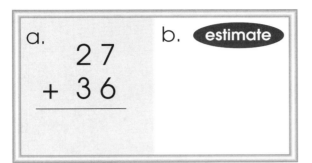

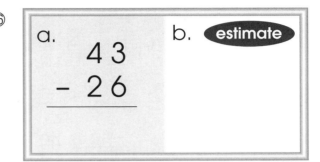

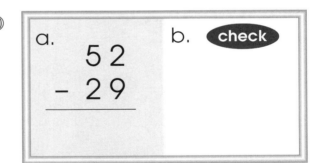

Complete.

35. $8 + 3\ \ \ = 10 + \text{\_\_\_\_\_} = \text{\_\_\_\_\_}$

36. $19 + 26 = 20 + \text{\_\_\_\_\_} = \text{\_\_\_\_\_}$

37. $13 + 29 = \text{\_\_\_\_\_} + 30 = \text{\_\_\_\_\_}$

38. $25 + 38 = \text{\_\_\_\_\_} + 40 = \text{\_\_\_\_\_}$

39. a. $9 - 6\ \ = \text{\_\_\_\_\_}$

    b. $19 - 6 = \text{\_\_\_\_\_}$

    c. $29 - 6 = \text{\_\_\_\_\_}$

    d. $39 - 6 = \text{\_\_\_\_\_}$

40. a. $62 - 9\ \ = \text{\_\_\_\_\_}$

    b. $62 - 19 = \text{\_\_\_\_\_}$

    c. $62 - 29 = \text{\_\_\_\_\_}$

    d. $62 - 39 = \text{\_\_\_\_\_}$

Fill in the numbers.

41.
$$\begin{array}{r} 4\ \square \\ +\ \square\ 9 \\ \hline 6\ 2 \end{array}$$

42.
$$\begin{array}{r} \square\ 8 \\ +\ 2\ \square \\ \hline 6\ 5 \end{array}$$

43.
$$\begin{array}{r} \square\ 5 \\ +\ 1\ \square \\ \hline 7\ 1 \end{array}$$

44.
$$\begin{array}{r} \square\ 2 \\ -\ 4\ \square \\ \hline 2\ 0 \end{array}$$

45.
$$\begin{array}{r} \square\ 1 \\ -\ 3\ \square \\ \hline 1\ 4 \end{array}$$

46.
$$\begin{array}{r} 5\ \square \\ -\ \square\ 3 \\ \hline 2\ 5 \end{array}$$

Find the answers.

㊼ 9 + 7 − 6 = ______

㊽ 5 + 7 + 8 = ______

㊾ 8 − 3 + 6 = ______

㊿ 7 + 2 − 4 = ______

(51) 69 − 23 + 17

= ______ + 17

= ______

(52) 14 + 35 − 26

= ______ − 26

= ______

(53) 22 + 36 − 49

= ______ − 49

= ______

(54) 72 − 58 + 13

= ______ + 13

= ______

The children are shopping. Put a ✓ in the ☐ to show what they buy.

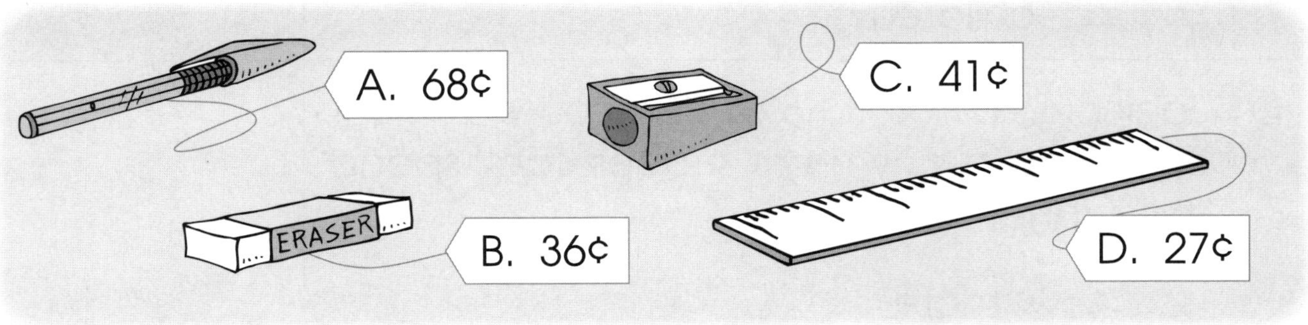
A. 68¢
C. 41¢
ERASER
B. 36¢
D. 27¢

(55) 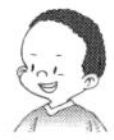 spends 77¢. He buys A B C D.

(56) 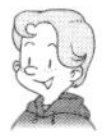 spends 63¢. He buys A B C D.

(57) 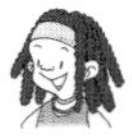 gets 32¢ change from 100¢. She buys A B C D.

Complete.

58	Mom buys 8 red 🌹 and 25 yellow 🌹. How many 🌹 does she buy in all? _____ 🌹 in all.	$\begin{array}{r} 8 \\ +25 \\ \hline \end{array}$
59	There are 23 girls and 19 boys on the school bus. How many children are there on the school bus altogether? _____ children altogether.	
60	Sue has 92¢. She spends 57¢ for a 🥫. How many ¢ does she have left? _____ ¢ left.	
61	There are 26 children in a class. 17 children are reading. How many children are not reading? _____ children.	
62	Jack buys a 🍫 for 69¢. Jane buys a 🍭 for 35¢. How many more ¢ does Jack spend than Jane? _____ ¢ more.	
63	There are 38 🧁 and 45 🍪 in a cake shop. How many 🧁 🍪 are there altogether in the cake shop? _____ 🧁 🍪 altogether.	

ANSWERS

1   Addition and Subtraction Facts to 20

2. 14	3. 8	4. 17	5. 18
6. 12			
7. 14	8. 5	9. 4	10. 14
11. 18	12. 11	13. 13	14. 13
15. 15	16. 13		
17. 7	18. 5	19. 12	20. 3
21. 6	22. 1	23. 2	24. 0
25. 4	26. 2		
27. +	28. –	29. +	30. –
31. –	32. +	33. –	34. –
35. –	36. +	37. +	38. –

39.

40.

41.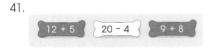

42.

43.

44a. 13	b. 14	c. 15	d. 16
45a. 9	b. 10	c. 11	d. 12
46. 12 + 6 ; 18 ; 18		47. 16 – 12 ; 4 ; 4	
48. 20 – 12 ; 8 ; 8		49. 10 + 5 ; 15 ; 15	

Just for Fun

2   More about Addition Facts

1b. 5	c. 5	
2a. 8	b. 8	c. 8
3a. 10	b. 10	c. 10
4a. 5	b. 5	c. 5
5a. 8	b. 8	c. 8
6. 3	7. 7	8. 4	9. 8
10. 7	11. 6	12. 6	13. 13
14. 6	15. 17	

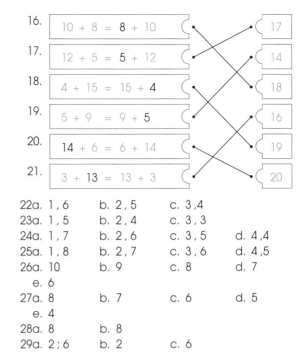

22a. 1 , 6	b. 2 , 5	c. 3 ,4	
23a. 1 , 5	b. 2 , 4	c. 3 , 3	
24a. 1 , 7	b. 2 , 6	c. 3 , 5	d. 4 ,4
25a. 1 , 8	b. 2 , 7	c. 3 , 6	d. 4 ,5
26a. 10	b. 9	c. 8	d. 7
e. 6			
27a. 8	b. 7	c. 6	d. 5
e. 4			
28a. 8	b. 8		
29a. 2 ; 6	b. 2	c. 6	

Just for Fun

2 ③ ⑧ 7 ⑥ ⑤ 4
④ ⑦ 5 ⑨ ② 3 6
6 9 ⑩ ① 4 ⑩

3   Relating Subtraction to Addition

1. 12 ; 4 ; 8   2. 18 ; 12
3. 15 ; 6   4. 17 ; 8
5. 11 ; 6
6. 6 ; 14 ; 8 ; 14 ; 6 ; 6
7. 5 , 6 ; 11 ; 6 , 5 ; 11 ; 11 , 6 ; 5 ; 11 , 5 ; 6
8. 4 , 9 ; 13 ; 9 , 4 ; 13 ; 13 , 4 ; 9 ; 13 , 9 ; 4
9. 12 , 7 ; 19 ; 7 , 12 ; 19 ; 19 , 7 ; 12 ; 19 , 12 ; 7
10. 7 , 9 ; 16 ; 9 , 7 ; 16 ; 16 , 7 ; 9 ; 16 , 9 ; 7
11. 11 , 6 ; 17 ; 6 , 11 ; 17 ; 17 , 11 ; 6 ; 17 , 6 ; 11

12. 5 ; 5	13. 7 ; 7	14. 9	15. 10
16. 7	17. 16	18. 11	19. 8
20. 7 ; 7	21. 3 ; 3		
22. 9 ; 9	23. 8 ; 8	24. 6 ; 6	25. 4 ; 4
26. 8 ; 8	27. 7 ; 7	28. 5 ; 5	29. 9 ; 9
30. 6 ; 6	31. 6 ; 6		

Just for Fun

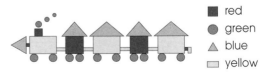

red
green
blue
yellow

4   Adding and Subtracting Using Counting

1. 23	2. 24	3. 21	4. 16
5. 24	6. 27	7. 22	8. 21

9. 19 10. 28 11. 18 12. 26
13. 29 14. 22 15. 26 16. 18
17. 30 18. 14
19. 57 20. 67 21. 58 22. 75
23. 72 24. 89 25. 86 26. 79
27. 66 28. 56
29. 61 30. 84 31. 79 32. 74
33. 88 34. 82 35. 55 36. 80
37a. 4 ; 24 b. 14 ; 24 38a. 6 ; 36 b. 16 ; 36
39a. 8 ; 48 b. 18 ; 48 40a. 5 ; 55 b. 15 ; 55
41a. 0 ; 40 b. 10 ; 40 42a. 0 ; 50 b. 10 ; 50
43. 10
44.
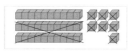

37 ; 10
45.

35 ; 21
46.
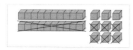

29 ; 13
47.
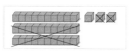

33 ; 11
48.
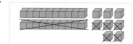

28 ; 13
49.
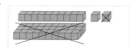

42 ; 11
50.
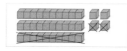

34 ; 22

Just for Fun

1.

2.

5 Adding without Regrouping I

1. 39
2.
```
   4 2
 +   4
 ─────
   4 6
```
3.
```
     4
 + 5 3
 ─────
   5 7
```
4.
```
   6 3
 +   5
 ─────
   6 8
```
5.
```
     6
 + 4 3
 ─────
   4 9
```
6. 29 7. 49 8. 38 9. 68
10. 57 11. 77 12. 89 13. 19
14. 38 15. 59 16. 67 17. 78
18. 48 19. 86 20. 29 21. 95
22. 16 23. 38 24. 68 25. 48
26. 27 27. 56 28. 27 29. 18
30. 38 31. 28 32. 66 33. 59
34. 48 35. 75 36. 87 37. 27
38. 96
39. policeman
40. 32 + 4 ; 36 ; 36 41. 20 + 6 ; 26 ; 26
42. 45 + 3 ; 48 ; 48 43. 23 + 6 ; 29 ; 29

Just for Fun

28 ; 27 ; 39 ; 19

6 Adding without Regrouping II

1. 57
2.
```
   2 2
 + 1 6
 ─────
   3 8
```
3.
```
   3 4
 + 1 4
 ─────
   4 8
```
4.
```
   2 0
 + 3 0
 ─────
   5 0
```
5. 38 6. 77 7. 67 8. 78
9. 67 10. 58 11. 91 12. 92
13. 47 14. 73 15. 78 16. 76
17. 93 18. 88 19. 46 20. 36
21. 44 22. 47 23. 86 24. 68
25. 86 26. 88 27. 59 28. 96
29. 47 30. 38 31. 59 32. 69
33. 57 34. 78 35. 88 36. 68
37. 99
38. 38 ; 47 ; 57 ; 59 ; 68 ; 69 ; 78 ; 88 ; 99
39. 44 + 32 ; 76 ; 76 40. 53 + 46 ; 99 ; 99
41. 22 + 36 ; 58 ; 58 42. 15 + 30 ; 45 ; 45

Just for Fun

7 Adding with Regrouping I

1. 32
2.
```
   4 6
 +   8
 ─────
   5 4
```
3.
```
   3 4
 +   9
 ─────
   4 3
```
4.
```
     6
 + 4 5
 ─────
   5 1
```
5. 24 6. 32 7. 40 8. 53
9. 65 10. 72 11. 28 12. 71
13. 83 14. 52 15. 36 16. 60
17. 44 18. 61 19. 56 20. 33
21. 61 22. 44 23. 51 24. 35

25. 70   26. 81   27. 94   28. 40
29. 43   30. 53   31. 35   32. 60
33. 72   34. 28   35. 83   36. 42
37. 34   38. 90   39. 61   40. 55
41. 70   42. 81
43. 18 + 6 ; 24 ; 24   44. 37 + 5 ; 42 ; 42
45. 28 + 8 ; 36 ; 36   46. 45 + 9 ; 54 ; 54

Just for Fun

8   Adding with Regrouping II

1. 43
2. 37 + 26 = 63
3. 35 + 17 = 52
4. 29 + 32 = 61
5. 56   6. 64   7. 70   8. 82
9. 80   10. 83   11. 91   12. 63
13. 85   14. 84   15. 71   16. 96
17. 92   18. 95   19. 60   20. 70
21. 83   22. 85   23. 81   24. 84
25. 93   26. 64   27. 82   28. 91

29.
30.
31.
32.
33.
34.
35.
36.

37. 15 + 9 ; 24 ; 24   38. 36 + 49 ; 85 ; 85
39. 54 + 38 ; 92 ; 92   40. 27 + 45 ; 72 ; 72

Just for Fun

6 ; 15 ; 28 ; 45 ; 66 ; 91

Midway Review

1. 7 ; 13   2. 5 ; 11   3. 9 ; 17   4. 9 ; 13
5. 7 ; 12   6. 8 ; 8   7. 8 ; 12   8. 11 ; 11
9a. 1 , 9   b. 2 , 8   c. 3 , 7   d. 4 , 6
e. 5 , 5
10a. 10   b. 9   c. 8   d. 7
e. 6
11. 7 ; 15 ; 8 ; 15 ; 7 ; 7
12. 3 , 10 ; 13 ; 10 , 3 ; 13 ; 13 , 3 ; 10 ; 13 , 10 ; 3
13. 6 ; 6   14. 6 ; 6   15. 13   16. 16
17. 7 ; 7   18. 8 ; 8   19. 21   20. 18
21. 9 ; 9   22. 7 ; 7
23. 24   24. 41   25. 40   26. 58
27. 11   28. 63   29. 93   30. 6
31. 50   32. 74   33. 90   34. 89
35. 28   36. 22   37. 30   38. 30
39. 79   40. 75   41. 62   42. 81
43. 49   44. 85   45. 56   46. 7
47. 60 ; 60
48. 58   49. 41   50. 39
48. 35 + 23 = 58   49. 25 + 16 = 41   50. 23 + 16 = 39

9   Subtracting without Regrouping I

1. 44
2. 39 − 3 = 36
3. 26 − 3 = 23
4. 54 − 2 = 52
5. 25 − 5 = 20
6. 31   7. 21   8. 43   9. 92
10. 52   11. 70   12. 82   13. 43
14. 66   15. 21   16. 55   17. 31
18. 72   19. 12   20. 93   21. 40
22. 50   23. 24   24. 32   25. 62
26. 71   27. 84   28. 91   29. 40
30. 44   31. 34   32. 53   33. 62
34. 50   35. 35   36. 81   37. 90
38. 21   39. 41   40. 81   41. 31
42. 63   43. 63   44. 52
45. 28 − 6 ; 22 ; 22
46. 59 − 5 ; 54 ; 54
47. 46 − 4 ; 42 ; 42
48. 37 − 3 ; 34 ; 34

Just for Fun

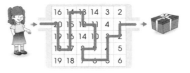

10 Subtracting without Regrouping II

1. 23
2.
```
  6 7
- 4 3
-----
  2 4
```
3.
```
  5 5
- 1 5
-----
  4 0
```
4.
```
  3 6
- 2 4
-----
  1 2
```

5. 24   6. 23   7. 24   8. 41
9. 32   10. 30   11. 31   12. 4
13. 21   14. 22   15. 12   16. 54
17. 15   18. 10   19. 4   20. 32
21. 23   22. 22   23. 46   24. 40
25. 11   26. 14   27. 16   28. 13
29a. 34   b. 23   c. 34 ; colour a and c
30a. 22   b. 23   c. 23 ; colour b and c
31a. 16   b. 26   c. 16 ; colour a and c
32a. 45   b. 45   c. 44 ; colour a and b
33. 16 ; 16   34. 24   35. 12   36. 32
```
  9 6        2 8        6 7
- 7 2      - 1 6      - 3 5
-----      -----      -----
  2 4        1 2        3 2
```

Just for Fun

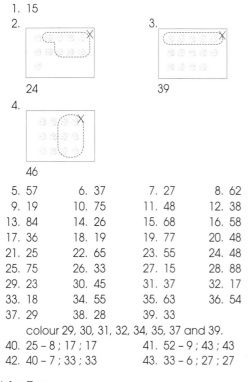

11 Subtracting with Regrouping I

1. 15
2.

24
3.

39
4.

46

5. 57   6. 37   7. 27   8. 62
9. 19   10. 75   11. 48   12. 38
13. 84   14. 26   15. 68   16. 58
17. 36   18. 19   19. 77   20. 48
21. 25   22. 65   23. 55   24. 48
25. 75   26. 33   27. 15   28. 88
29. 23   30. 45   31. 37   32. 17
33. 18   34. 55   35. 63   36. 54
37. 29   38. 28   39. 33
colour 29, 30, 31, 32, 34, 35, 37 and 39.
40. 25 – 8 ; 17 ; 17   41. 52 – 9 ; 43 ; 43
42. 40 – 7 ; 33 ; 33   43. 33 – 6 ; 27 ; 27

Just for Fun

54 ; 42 ; 29 ; 15 ; 0

12 Subtracting with Regrouping II

1. 26
2.

14
3.

18
4. 16   5. 38   6. 16   7. 45
8. 18   9. 28   10. 8   11. 29
12. 17   13. 19   14. 37   15. 27
16. 16   17. 13   18. 9   19. 28
20. 17   21. 28   22. 25   23. 37
24. 47   25. 23   26. 12   27. 26
28a. 36   b. 23   c. 36 ; colour a and c
29a. 27   b. 37   c. 37 ; colour b and c
30a. 14   b. 14   c. 15 ; colour a and b
31a. 26   b. 25   c. 25 ; colour b and c
32a. 44   b. 34   c. 44 ; colour a and c
33. 92 – 37 ; 55 ; 55
34. 43 – 27 ; 16 ; 16
35. 55 – 39 ; 16 ; 16
36. 61 – 46 ; 15 ; 15

Just for Fun

SINGER

13 Estimating Sums and Differences

1. 30   2. 40   3. 50   4. 40
5. 60   6. 80   7. 80   8. 90
9. 40   10. 20
11. 30   12. 20   13. 50   14. 60
15. 10   16. 80   17. 10   18. 50
19. 10   20. 70   21. 100   22. 0
23a. 66   b. 70
24a. 44   25a. 53
  b.   b.
```
    2 0                  1 0
  + 3 0                + 5 0
  -----                -----
    5 0                  6 0
```
26a. 65   27a. 33
  b.   b.
```
    5 0                  3 0
  + 1 0                + 1 0
  -----                -----
    6 0                  4 0
```
28a. 89
  b.
```
    3 0
  + 6 0
  -----
    9 0
```
29a. 92   b. 70 , 20 ; 90
30a. 88   b. 20 , 70 ; 90
31a. 79   b. 30 , 50 ; 80
32a. 95   b. 50 , 40 ; 90
33a. 91   b. 60 , 30 ; 90
34a. 58   b. 10 , 50 ; 60
35a. 24   b. 20

36a. 15

b.

```
   40
 - 20
 ───
   20
```

37a. 32

b.

```
   70
 - 40
 ───
   30
```

38a. 26

b.

```
   70
 - 50
 ───
   20
```

39a. 41

b.

```
   60
 - 10
 ───
   50
```

40a. 36

b.

```
   90
 - 50
 ───
   40
```

41a. 47   b. 90 , 50 ; 40
42a. 33   b. 50 , 10 ; 40
43a. 48   b. 80 , 30 ; 50
44a. 45   b. 60 , 20 ; 40
45a. 48   b. 80 , 30 ; 50
46a. 28   b. 40 , 10 ; 30
48. less than 80
49. more than 90
50. less than 20
51. less than 40
52. more than 70

Just for Fun

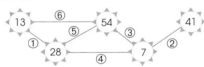

14 Checking Subtraction by Using Addition

1a. 12   b. 12 ; 28
2a. 26   b. 26 ; 63
3a. 22   b. 22 ; 48
4a. 18   b. 18 ; 51
5a. 35   b. 35 ; 77
6a. 23   b. 23 ; 82
7a. 44   b. 44 , 8 ; 52
8a. 22   b. 22 , 17 ; 39
9a. 22   b. 22 , 23 ; 45
10a. 27   b. 27 , 39 ; 66
11a. 42   b. 42 , 45 ; 87
12a. 7   b. 7 , 16 ; 23
13a. 38   b. 38 , 33 ; 71
14a. 35   b. 35 , 63 ; 98
15a. 18   b. 18 , 14 ; 32
16a. 21   b. 21 , 6 ; 27
17a. 25   b. 25 , 31 ; 56
18a. 16   b. 16 , 29 ; 45
19a. 39   b. 39   c. 39
20a. 21   b. 21 , 17 ; 38   c. 38 , 21 ; 17
21a. 17   b. 17 , 32 ; 49   c. 49 , 17 ; 32
22a. 26   b. 26 , 25 ; 51   c. 51 , 26 ; 25
23a. 13   b. 13 , 9 ; 22   c. 22 , 13 ; 9

24a. 71   b. 71 , 15 ; 86   c. 86 , 71 ; 15
25a. 25   b. 25 , 65 ; 90   c. 90 , 25 ; 65
26a. 27   b. 27 , 48 ; 75   c. 75 , 27 ; 48
27. 56 , 39 ; 17 ; 17

```
   17
 + 39
 ───
   56
```

28. 48 , 26 ; 22 ; 22

```
   22
 + 26
 ───
   48
```

29. 15 , 8 ; 7 ; 7

```
    7
 +  8
 ───
   15
```

Just for Fun

1. 20 ; 35 ; 45
2. 40 ; 44 ; 46
3. 40 ; 50 ; 80

15 More Addition and Subtraction

1. 9 ; 6   2. 2 ; 10   3. 14 ; 5   4. 6 ; 12
5. 16 ; 2   6. 35 ; 29   7. 82 ; 80   8. 29 ; 36
9. 70 ; 52   10. 80 ; 34
12. 60   13. 36   14. 46   15. 36
16. 46   17. 13
18. 24 ; 44   19. 32 ; 62   20. 33 ; 53   21. 14 ; 54
22. 2 ; 12
23. 20 ; 40   24. 20 ; 40   25. 14 ; 44   26. 12 ; 42
27. 30   28. 10   29. 44   30. 40
31. 43   32. 20   33. 30   34. 26
35. 30   36. 18   37. 20   38. 30
39a. 3   b. 13   c. 23   d. 33
e. 43
40a. 6   b. 16   c. 26   d. 36
e. 46
41a. 64   b. 54   c. 44   d. 34
e. 24
42a. 58   b. 48   c. 38   d. 28
e. 18
43. 8 + 4 - 5 ; 7
44. 9 - 3 + 5 ; 11
45. 7 + 6 - 4 ; 9

Just for Fun

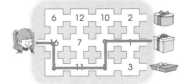

16 Addition and Subtraction with Money

1. 65   2. 42   3. 52   4. 37
5. 28
7. ✓

8. 50 , 49 ; 1　　　　9. 100 , 85 ; 15
10. 45 , 36 ; 9　　　　11. 75 , 56 ; 19
12. 67 , 36 ; 31　　　13. 76 , 46 ; 30
14. 72 , 47 ; 25　　　15. 28 , 16 ; 12

	25¢	10¢	5¢	1¢
16.	2			4
17.		2		2
18.	3		1	
19.	1	2		2
20.	1	1		1

21. 57　　22. 66　　23. 32　　24. 41
25. 34 ; 34
26. 98
```
    57
 + 41
   98
```
27. 89
```
    57
 + 32
   89
```
28. 34
```
    66
 - 32
   34
```
29. 25
```
    66
 - 41
   25
```

Just for Fun

2 , 4

Final Review

1. 41　　2. 45　　3. 32　　4. 43
5. 28　　6. 18　　7. 57　　8. 66
9. 71　　10. 55　　11. 80　　12. 19
13. 36　　14. 69　　15. 43　　16. 70
17. 73　　18. 27　　19. 16　　20. 91
21. 56　　22. 42　　23. 25　　24. 49
25a. 63　　　　　　26a. 17
b.
```
    30
 + 40
   70
```
b.
```
    40
 - 30
   10
```
27a. 26　　b. 70 – 40 ; 30
28a. 58　　b. 40 + 20 ; 60
29a. 23　　　　　　30a. 23
b.
```
    23
 + 14
   37
```
b.
```
    23
 + 29
   52
```
31a. 16　　b. 16 + 48 ; 64
32a. 46　　b. 46 + 33 ; 79
33a. 32　　b. 32 + 54 ; 86
34a. 25　　b. 25 + 28 ; 53
35. 1 ; 11　　36. 25 ; 45　　37. 12 ; 42　　38. 23 ; 63
39a. 3　　b. 13　　c. 23　　d. 33
40a. 53　　b. 43　　c. 33　　d. 23
41.
```
   4 3
 + 1 9
   6 2
```
42.
```
   3 8
 + 2 7
   6 5
```
43.
```
   5 5
 + 1 6
   7 1
```

44.
```
   6 2
 - 4 2
   2 0
```
45.
```
   5 1
 - 3 7
   1 4
```
46.
```
   5 8
 - 3 3
   2 5
```
47. 8　　48. 20　　49. 11　　50. 5
51. 46 ; 63　　52. 49 ; 23　　53. 58 ; 9　　54. 14 ; 27
55. B ; C　　56. B ; D　　57. A
58. 33 ; 33
59. 42　　60. 35　　61. 9　　62. 34
```
    23
 + 19
   42
```
```
    92
 - 57
   35
```
```
    26
 - 17
    9
```
```
    69
 - 35
   34
```
63. 83
```
    38
 + 45
   83
```